No Fairy Godmothers, No Magic Wands:

The Healing Process After Rape

BY JUDITH H. KATZ

R&E Publishers
Saratoga, California

R & E Publishers
P.O. Box 2008, Saratoga, CA 95070
Tel: (408) 866-6303   Fax: (408) 866-0825

Library of Congress Card Catalog Number: 82-61474

ISBN *0-88247-990-3*

Dedicated to all Women in our

Struggle to be Free

CONTENTS

PREFACE

This book is about rape and about me. I am a rape victim. My intention is to share with you that experience which has affected my whole being, changed my perceptions, my self-concept, and altered many of my personal relationships. I will relate an experience filled with horror and violence so that you may understand the trauma of being physically and emotionally violated. It's not my intention to frighten you. My purpose is to discuss rape, its effects and the consequences of the assault on significant people in my life. If you are a victim of rape, you will probably understand and be able to relate to the story that unfolds on the pages that follow; it is my hope that it will ease your burden and help you feel somewhat less alone in your own struggle to integrate the rape into your life. If you are not a rape victim, perhaps this book will make you more aware of the pain and suffering which rape victims experience.

Unless you are a victim, it is extremely difficult to understand the impact of rape. If you are in the fields of mental health, or if you are a family member, spouse or friend of a victim, this book is written with the intent of providing you insight into the ordeal.

In day-to-day situations, rape is often joked about by both men and women. Other people may wonder how a woman could get herself into such a situation, or how she could have provoked the attack. They may even wonder whether she enjoyed the experience. Others may question the inability of a woman to put the trauma behind her six months, twelve months, or even three years later. What these individuals do not understand about rape is, of course, the reality of the assault itself. Rape cuts to the core of a woman's existence. It is not a crime of passion, lust or sexuality, but one of violence.

The difficulty in understanding the effects of such an experience on women is analogous to the paradox experienced in trying to understand the effects of the Vietnam War on returning veterans. Those men who fought in Vietnam know the feelings of fear and alienation. They know how impossible it is to describe what occurred and how difficult it is to talk about its effect on their lives. Many men have repressed their feelings, denied their emotions and attempted to block the experience. Still others feel shame and internalize their anger. The emotional turmoil and pain each man suffers is both unique and yet common to Vietnam veterans.

In much the same way, rape victims understand one another. Each woman's experience is a personal one and, at the same time, very universal. Those individuals who have not had such an experience remain somewhat alienated from the victim. An abyss is created which must be bridged with understanding.

Over the past fifteen years, more attention has been drawn to this serious issue. Authors such as Brownmiller, Burgess and Holmstrom have focused the nation's attention on the reality of rape. They have made the issue a political and a societal concern.

Professional women and men are speaking out concerning the needs of the victim. Medical professionals, legal and police personnel and counselors are all seriously involved in changing the outdated treatment and care that rape victims receive.

This book describes in detail my experience of being raped and the impact that it has had on my personal and professional life. The rape not only changed my life and my impressions and reactions to the world around me, but it also altered the lives of my closest friends and immediate family. In my struggle to incorporate the rape into my life, I found that my feminist convictions played a major role in the healing process. As a feminist, I see rape as a socio-political dominated issue. We, as women, are not free. Although our country preaches freedom and equality, the fact that women cannot walk on the streets or sleep safely in their own homes is just one small example of the inequalities women experience. Rape is only one form of violence against women. Through the educational process, media and legislation, women and men have learned that women are second class citizens. We are not only the brunt of jokes but also the objects of men's frustration, anger and violence. The social, political and economic inequality that women experience necessitates our standing up for what we believe and feel as women. We have suffered in our silence for too long, I have, therefore, chosen not to remain silent about being sexually assaulted. I recognize a need to reach out and develop awareness around me. My feminist convictions, coupled with my professional work as a counselor and human relations practitioner, have enabled me to channel my hostility and negative behaviors into more positive endeavors. In an effort to regain a sense of power and safety, I have sought every opportunity to make people aware of my experience and the toll it has taken on my life. I have also attempted to use my professional position as a way to enlighten others as to the reality of rape and the needs of rape victims. In the courses that I teach in counseling and human relations, I address the needs of rape victims and how counselors can help both a rape victim and significant others to deal with the aftermath of the rape. In addition, I do a great deal of speaking to various community and university groups about the impact of rape on a woman's life and the reality of rape in our "nice college" community.

The healing process has not been an easy one. Although I had much assistance after being raped to deal with my reactions to the rape, my emotional state was still unstable. No amount of cognitive understanding could make the feelings dissipate. At times, I attempted to repress my emotions and at other times, to completely deny them. There were days when I wished the experience would vanish into outer space. I looked for easy cures and temporary relief. And yet, no matter how frantically I searched for my fairy godmother with her magic wand, the pain remained. I had to experience the traumas and aftermath of rape. In retrospect, I wonder whether if not for my support group I would have made the journey back at all, or remained emotionally crippled for the rest of my life as a result of the rape.

Over the past years I have kept a journal of my reactions and thoughts. This is one way I sorted through my feelings. I have included excerpts from this journal as a way to share the range of emotions and frustrations I experienced. Excerpts of letters from friends are also included, as a way to describe the impact of the rape on their lives, too.

I have written this book with the awareness that some of what I describe is unique to my own experience. Yet, I am also aware that much of what I cover is universal to other rape victims. When I publicly speak to groups about rape, I hear many women indicating similar responses to their own situations. Similar effects have also been confirmed through my development of and work with a rape support group for rape victims in the community. What has been so startling and disheartening throughout this process is how many women whom I know had been victims of rape at some point in their life. It was only when I shared my experience openly that they felt permission to discuss this locked away part of themselves. I have, therefore, attempted to capture not only my own thoughts and feelings but also the collective experience of other women who have been raped.

You may find as you read this book that you will react in various ways to what is described. You may find yourself questioning my reactions or feeling plagued with lingering myths that cloud your ability to see rape as an act of violence. This may indicate some learning which needs to be done before you can adequately be of assistance to a woman who is a victim of rape. Many people do not consciously desire to impede the healing process but even the most subtle reactions and statements can be extremely damaging to a woman healing from being raped. Therefore, helpers, family members and friends must be very clear about their own attitudes and assumptions about rape. This book is written in an effort to clarify and describe the reality of rape so that we may all better understand how to help a victim of rape.

This book could not have been written without the help and support of my friends and family. To name all those people who have helped me through this crisis and enabled me to write this book is impossible. The honesty, caring, openness of those individuals cannot be adequately served in a few short lines; but several must be mentioned.

My heartfelt thanks go first to Nancy Meneely, who through her love and willingness to talk about her own pain of being raped, enabled me to give myself permission to address my own.

To Kris Libbee, who both personally and professionally has given me the support and encouragement to continue dealing with my feelings and writing this book. She is a sister in every meaning of the word.

To Andrea Wilson and Linda Barbie, part of my support group, who were always there when I needed them. They continually utilized their skills and learning as counselors and caring human beings.

To Carolyn Morgan, a friend and colleague, who encouraged me to go on speaking about rape and giving me the reassurance that this project was, in fact, necessary.

To Denise Fynmore, co-facilitator of the rape group, for her willingness to coordinate the group and coax me to work with her and for remaining a friend throughout.

To Rosalie Taylor and Anne Lowrance for sharing their professional experiences and expertise in working with rape victims and significant others.

To Cathy Zarlingo, who spent hours typing and re-typing this manuscript. Her support and concern for perfection helped to make this book a reality.

To my parents for their willingness to confront their own feelings and help me deal with mine. Their constant love is acknowledged and appreciated.

And, to Cresencio Torres for being one of the few men who not only cared enough to listen and support me but also helped me complete this book. His commitment as a partner and a friend was demonstrated through his willingness to edit this manuscript and in being there when the feelings connected with writing this book became overwhelming.

This book is the result of these people and many others who have touched my life and enabled me to find the fairy godmother within me to survive the ordeal of rape.

CHAPTER I

BEING A WOMAN MEANS
NOT BEING FREE: THE RAPE

September 13, 1976. I was lying in bed dozing somewhere between wakefulness and a deep, sound sleep. Suddenly I was startled awake by a hand placed tightly over my mouth and by a voice saying, "Don't scream or I'll kill you." At first I thought I was dreaming. It was dark in the room but I could see the clock from my bed. It was 1:00 a.m. Could this be real? Was there actually a man in my bedroom? I was in total disbelief and shock. Somehow this only happened to other women. How could this be happening to me? Then it hit me—in fact this situation was all too real. I felt myself panic. My stomach turned into a knot. Terror swept over my body. There was a man, a stranger, in my home. He was in my bedroom with his hand over my mouth! Questions flooded my head. Who was this man? How did he get in? What did he want from me? As these questions filled my mind, my fears increased and magnified. The final question, what was he going to do to me, could not be answered. Would he rape me? Would he kill me? Would I be cut up and maimed for life? My head was swimming in confusion. I wondered if I could ever speak to my friends and family again. I wondered what I had done to this man for him to want revenge. At that moment, I somehow felt personally responsible for his being there. What had I done to him?

What had I done to deserve this treatment? I realized, then, that my terror was taking hold of me. I attempted to regain control of myself.

As the seconds passed, he removed his hand from my mouth. I decided to see if I could talk to him. Perhaps I could engage him in a conversation. If I could find out more about him, become less of an object and more of a person, perhaps he'd leave me alone. I couldn't face the possibility that this man was going to rape or kill me. I asked him, "Why me?" He answered, "I've seen you around." I wondered silently where he had seen me since I had only lived in Oklahoma for three weeks. I was struck by his voice. He had a deep Oklahoma accent. I was keenly aware of it since my New York ears were not yet used to the sound. His voice was gruff and very distinctive. I would never forget that sound.

I was relieved that he had replied to my question. I thought that my strategy might work. I envisioned that this man had deep psychological problems. I hoped that I could talk him out of raping me. Unfortunately, this was not the case. Undoubtedly, I had watched too many television movies where the rapist just wants someone to understand him. My wanting to find out more about him, hoping he just needed a friendly ear, was my way to hold on to some power in a very powerless and terrifying situation.

Hoping to get a dialogue started, I continued my questions. I asked him if he had ever had a meaningful relationship with a woman. He replied, "Yes." My hopes rose a little higher. Attempting to strike some chord of humanity in this man, I stated, "Obviously this isn't meaningful for either of us." There was no response. I felt disheartened. I tried another approach. I attempted an appeal to some sense of compassion or conscience. I asked him if he realized all the trauma that this was going to cause. He responded by telling me to shut up. I felt defeated.

In retrospect, the conversation was more for me than for him. I needed to hear my voice to know that I was still alive and breathing. I needed a strategy—a way, some way to deal with this man. It was apparent that the rapist cared little about my feelings, mental health or well being. Talking to him was the only way I knew of using my skills in counseling and human relations. I hoped my being a "fast talker" from New York would help. It didn't. As our one-sided dialogue ended, my fears and anxieties grew. What would happen next?

Up until this point, he had not violated me. I was still lying in bed on my stomach with the covers protecting me. He then pulled the covers off. I lay there naked, feeling incredibly vulnerable. Never in my life had I felt so exposed. Thoughts raced through my head once again. I felt guilty for not wearing a nightgown. I felt like an open target. How would it sound in court? I imagined the defense attorney asking me leading questions about why I slept nude. I began prosecuting myself.

I blamed myself for leaving the study window open. If only I had used my New York survival skills. In New York, I would never have lived in a first floor apartment and most definitely would not have left a window open. I felt guilty for not listening to my mother's advice about taking a second floor apartment. I heard her blaming me and telling me that she had warned me. But I had thought, perhaps assumed, that Oklahoma was different from New York. I still could not believe this was happening to me. I had been on top of the world until now. The rapist crawled into bed beside me. It was then that I realized he, too, was naked. My world crumbled around me.

He told me to spread my legs. I thought for a second about following his commands. He began stroking my thighs. I felt my whole body tense as he touched me. I was repulsed by his touch, yet surprised that his hands were soft and gentle. Part of me wanted so desperately to fight back but I feared retaliation. I decided to try and struggle with him to see how he would react. Maybe I could get free? My struggling only made him angry. He warned me to behave myself or he would have to hurt me. The struggle left me in a more vulnerable position. Whereas before, I lay stomach down, my back sheltering me from him, I was now, after the struggle, lying on my back feeling fully exposed. The dehumanization process took yet another step.

I was filled with more fear and terror. I thought that I was going to die. I was unsure whether or not he had a weapon. But I also knew, whether he did or not, that he could kill me just the same. I kept on telling myself to try and focus on what he felt like so that I could give that information to the police if and when he left. I repeated over and over again to myself that I would call the police and two of my friends, Jan and Andrea, as soon as I could. I kept hoping that I would be alive to make those calls. I kept on thinking about what I would do in case he left so as not to deal with my feelings of powerlessness and fright at that moment.

He slid down and performed cunninlingus. I fantasized somehow defecating in his face. At this point I had the first opportunity to see his face. However, I didn't look. I thought he would kill me if I could identify him.

I raged inside and kept calm outside. I tried to rationalize the situation. I told myself that I had been sexually involved with men before when I didn't want to be. I remembered a time when I had intercourse and really didn't want to, but acquiesced because it seemed easier than hassling and saying no. For a moment, I tried to convince myself that this was the same type of experience. But it wasn't! This was incredibly different. I had no rights. I was an object. I had no power, no knowledge of what was to happen, no sense of whether I'd be dead or alive, no information as to who this stranger was or what he was going to do or how long he was going to stay. I didn't have my body. I was totally under his control. This was not sex—it was an invasion.

His penis attempted to enter my vagina but was unable to do so. I lay there stiff, passive, motionless. I felt alienated and humiliated. I attempted to psychologically block what

4

was happening to me physically. I found myself disassociating my body from my mind. I kept my focus on calling the police. I silently repeated over and over what I'd do after he left.

I grew more anxious as he continued having difficulty getting an erection. At this point, I just wanted him to get it over with and leave me alone. I feared that he would require me to become an active participant. My terror increased as each moment passed. Fearing that he would get violent if he could not reach his goal, I put my hand on his shoulder and told him that he was okay. It was the reassurance that he needed. I then hated myself for encouraging him. Once again, I imagined the courtroom scene. The attorney was accusing me of helping the rapist. But, I argued with myself that I feared for my life if he couldn't meet his goal. It was a question of survival. At this point, I had one purpose in mind—to stay alive. It was the only thing in my power to do.

His penis entered me and he had an orgasm. My immediate response was relief that it was over but then I realized that I did not know what would happen next. Now that he had raped me, would he kill me? Would he stay all night? Was this the end or just the beginning?

Each second that he lay on top of me felt like an eternity. Finally, he got up and told me to stay there for five minutes. I dared not open my eyes. I wondered if he was leaving or returning to kill me.

Struck with indecision, I didn't know if I should follow his command. I thought about jumping out of the bedroom window screaming for help, or fortifying the bedroom door in case he returned, or putting on the bedroom lights. I jumped out of bed in an attempt to lock the bedroom door. As I did this, I watched the man walk out my front door, naked. I saw that he was about 5 feet 5 inches tall, with sandy brown hair. I captured that image as information for the police.

I ran to lock the door (not realizing his fingerprints

were probably there). I turned on every light in the apartment and put on a robe. Immediately I called the police and the two friends that I had thought about throughout the rape. I stood in my apartment shaking, not knowing what to do, waiting for someone to arrive. I prayed that I would be safe during the interim. I looked at the clock. It was 1:20 a.m. All of this had taken place in only twenty minutes. In that time period, I had gone from feeling that I was a confident, powerful woman, to feeling like a helpless, dehumanized object. Not only had I been raped, but I felt stripped of my dignity. In disbelief and shock, I repeated over and over, "I've been raped." The events of the past twenty minutes became surreal.

I thought about the two women I had called for help. One woman was a colleague of mine at the University. Although we knew each other only a short period of time, she had generously extended herself to me in my move from Amherst, where I completed my doctoral work, to Oklahoma where I would begin my career as a professor at the University. Jan had opened up her home to me on several occasions and had been a support system. I felt I could rely on her. I thought it ironic that as I drove home from her house earlier that evening I had figured out how long it took to get from her part of town to my apartment.

Andrea was called for different reasons. She was a graduate student in my department. We had met three weeks before and found some commonalities—both of us were Jewish and from New York City. She had worked in a rape crisis center while living in New York City. We had talked about working together on developing a better rape response program in Norman. Little did we know at that time that her knowledge and expertise would be necessary so soon and so personally. I called Andrea, assuming she could assure that appropriate procedures were followed. She'd know what to do and how to help me. When I called her and told her that I had been raped, she was in shock. Helping rape victims who are strangers is one thing but when it is someone you know, it's quite different. Her first response when I called and told her what happened was, "You're kidding." Obviously, I was never more serious. She then realized the gravity of the situation and was on her way.

Holding myself together both physically and emotionally, I paced the apartment waiting for help. Although the physical rape was now over, the trauma and emotional assault had just begun.

CHAPTER II

THE HOURS AFTER: POLICE, HOSPITAL AND IMMEDIATE NEEDS

I swore to myself that if I was ever raped I would never deal with a male police officer. My convictions told me that men just couldn't understand the experience. I assumed that I would be so angry I would want to kill the first man that I saw. I was to learn that my assumption was, in fact, inaccurate when faced with the reality of being raped.

The first person to arrive at my apartment was a young male police officer. I met him at the door with skepticism and mistrust. I was prepared for his comments to be sexist and blaming. But, surprisingly, I found myself relieved by his presence. There was now someone else in the apartment—I felt safe. The rapist would not return.

The officer was young and appeared nervous and rather inexperienced. I found myself taking control of the situation. I asked him questions about what I should do. Should I get dressed? What information did he need? He informed me that a detective would ask for all the details of the assault. As I showed him around the apartment, he asked that I not touch anything because the police would be dusting the apartment for fingerprints later. At that moment, my friends arrived.

Jan expressed her relief seeing that I was not physically

abused. She anticipated finding me beaten and bruised. Andrea, on the other hand, had no such image because of her previous experience with rape victims. Outwardly I appeared calm although in reality I was in severe shock. I controlled my emotions for fear that if I didn't I would become hysterical.

As Jan and Andrea drove me to the hospital, I calmly talked about the events that had occurred less than an hour before. Part of me wondered if the rape really happened and the other part of me knew all too well that it did. I tried to deny it.

At the hospital, I became aware of a strong feeling of distrust. With the new individuals I encountered, I wondered what their reactions would be to me as a rape victim. Support became critical at this point. No one could be neutral in my eyes. I had to know if others would accept me. The only way I could be certain was to carefully observe their reactions towards me.

The first person that I encountered was the emergency room nurse. Her responses were cold and clinical as she showed me to one of the rooms. I was then asked to fill out a battery of forms. It seemed that her concern focused not on my health but on how the hospital would be paid. I had a difficult time answering the questions. Even trying to remember my address and phone number seemed an overwhelming task. I classified the nurse as an adversary. She demonstrated no warmth or empathy toward me. Undoubtedly, she was having a difficult time dealing with me as a rape victim. Since there was no physical injury, perhaps she doubted that I was raped? Perhaps rape was too threatening for her to deal with at the time. I hoped that she would, at least, explain the procedures that I would follow during the examination but she kept me totally in the dark. She gave me no information. I felt even more powerless. I waited in the cold cubicle alone, not knowing how long I would be there or with whom I would deal. I wondered when I would see the police detective or a physician. Once again, my life and fate were in the hands of someone else. I felt that I had no control in this situation. Again, I felt more like an object than a person. I was not a woman who had been raped. I was just the "rape victim."

Andrea finally joined me in the room after what seemed like a long time of sitting alone. It was in her presence that I began to allow my feelings and thoughts to surface. I felt safe with her. I trusted that she had some understanding of my feelings because of her experience with rape victims I began to give myself permission to stop controlling my emotions. Andrea gave me support and reassurances I needed. She held my hand as she encouraged me to express my feelings.

My first statements were of continued disbelief. I repeated, "I can't believe I was raped." I still didn't believe that this could happen to me. Somehow I felt that I could avoid being raped. I started wondering if perhaps I had in some way set up the rape. I then felt ashamed with myself for internalizing this myth about rape. In som many ways I was trying to deny what had actually taken place. I had been raped. When the realization hit me, I burst into tears. I sat on the examination table crying and shaking. Andrea gave me encouraging words of comfort and caring. She continually gave me permission to experience what I was feeling. I started recounting to her the events that took place but this time the emotional impact became obvious. I kept on repeating, "If only I had not left my window open . . . If only I had taken a second floor apartment." I was feeling guilty, blaming myself and feeling responsible for the rape. Andrea reassured me that I was not to blame. Cognitively, I knew she was right but emotionally I continued to feel that I might have been able to do something else to avoid the rape.

Finally, the detective arrived. Andrea was asked to leave the room. A male detective in his early thirties entered. He was about 5'7", with a medium build. His small size made him seem less of a threat. However, I was still extremely suspicious. I was angry that the one female detective on the police force was unavailable that night. At this point, I did not want to deal with any more men. My defenses were high as I anticipated a male's blaming tone of voice, accusatory questions and judgmental responses. How could he understand? I listened cautiously as he introduced himself. He appeared surprisingly warm and concerned. He gave me information about the questioning that was to follow. Also, he gave me permission to take my time and cry if needed. He did this by demonstrating empathy and some understanding about how painful the experience was for me. I classified him as a person who would be supportive. I was eased by his calm voice and manner. The fact that he did not have an Oklahoma accent was also a relief. I associated an Oklahoma accent with the rapist. I felt safe with the detective — I trusted him.

I calmly recalled in detail the events of the rape. I found myself making jokes as a way of dealing with my anxiety and discomfort. I laughed as I told the detective that it was ironic that I had lived in New York for twenty-two years and nothing had ever happened to me. Here I was in Oklahoma for only three weeks and I was raped. I asked him if that was Oklahoma's way of welcoming people from out of state. I expected him to respond negatively when I told him that I had left my study window open. I joked about putting my hand on the rapist's shoulder. I was such a good human relations instructor that I comforted a man who was dehumanizing me. Again, I waited for a judgmental response and none came.

As I related the events, I felt guilty, shameful and lonely. I found it incredibly difficult to describe the rape itself. Although, usually not at a loss for words, it was tedious to describe the rapist's behavior explicitly. I found myself feeling uncomfortable describing in detail every word and action that the rapist took and every response I had to his actions. I silently wondered if the detective believed me. As I recounted the event, I felt enraged the more I thought about how a stranger could enter my life and have such a great impact on me. Not only was I the one raped, but now I was the one sitting in the hospital dealing with the police. I was really a victim in more ways than one. I would have to go to the police station the next day and fill out a formal written statement. They would fingerprint me to see if they could find the rapist's fingerprints at my apartment. I felt more the criminal and less the victim. The interview with the detective concluded and he left the room. As he left, I had a feeling that he believed me, and I was reassured that he would do what he could to try and apprehend the rapist. I had assured him that I would to to trial if the individual was caught. There was a glimmer of hope that something might be done. Most importantly, the detective wasn't blaming or accusatory. Now, if I could only stop blaming myself.

It was now 3:00 a.m. and I was once again sitting alone in that room after describing the rape in such detail and reliving those events. I felt abandoned. An immense sense of loneliness and alienation came over me. I felt that no one could understand what I had just experienced. I realized my mortality. I realized that I could have been killed. I didn't want to sit there by myself but I felt too helpless to walk outside the room and ask one of my friends to sit with me. I sat on the table shaking and sobbing. I felt that I had lost important parts of myself—my faith, my trust and my sense of security. I no longer felt that I had control of my life. I had a suspicion that I would never be the same again.

Finally, Andrea came into the emergency room. I was grateful that she was there. The nurse had been rather obstinate about allowing her to be in the room with me; however, Andrea insisted. She asked me if I wanted a cup of coffee. I refused the offer. She brought the cup of coffee anyway. It obviously was her way to feel useful. In retrospect, I would see how this kind of behavior increased my feelings of powerlessness. Again, my control had been taken from me. I was offered a choice about whether or not I wanted coffee. I made the decision not to have coffee and that decision was ignored by Andrea. In a very subtle way, what happened reinforced my present condition. I couldn't even make a decision without someone overriding me. However, it was easier for me to be angry with Andrea than to deal with my real anger at being disempowered.

Andrea attempted to help me by putting her experience into practice. Her major role was in helping me identify my needs and in helping me make up my mind about what to do after I left the hospital. She reassured me that I was safe. We discussed some options as to where I would spend the rest of that evening and the next few days. It was difficult to think about the future because I was so caught up in the rape itself. Throughout this decision-making process, I continued telling Andrea about parts of the rape experience. I needed to talk and to some degree test her reactions to what I said. Instead of confirming the negative feelings that I had about myself, she supported my actions during the rape. She encouraged me to think about the fact that I had survived. Andrea tried to find ways to help me regain confidence in myself. Her candidness about her reactions to my experience was extremely helpful. She also enabled me to make decisions about what I was going to do. I regained some feelings of power and I was determined to act on that resolve.

Andrea shared with me valuable information about the procedures the doctor would follow. In New York, Andrea had worked side by side with the physician. As a rape crisis worker, also known as a rape advocate, she was permitted to stay in the room and be of assistance to the victim. The advocate serves as an important bridge between the medical staff and the rape victim. By sharing information with the woman about what the doctor would do in the examination, and why, the advocate for the victim assists the woman to feel more control over her body. The advocate's use of information-sharing takes some of the power out of the doctor's hands and places it in the victim's. Oklahoma, at that time, did not have such a program; therefore, I was thankful that Andrea gave me some information about what might occur.

The doctor finally arrived followed by the nurse who

13

had ushered me into the room earlier. Andrea was asked again to leave. I wanted her to stay particularly given my feelings about the nurse, but I said nothing. I was physically and emotionally exhausted. It was now 3:30 in the morning. I wondered why it had taken the doctor so long to arrive? I already had very negative feelings about the nurse so the doctor's lateness did little to make me feel any better about him. My anxiety increased as I wondered what would occur in this next episode. I just wanted to get out of the hospital, take a shower and find some peace.

The doctor appeared annoyed. Apparently, he was awakened and called to the hospital. He was the only physician at the hospital trained to do the legal-medical examination. Special procedures must be followed so that the evidence could be admissible in court. I knew that I needed him but I resented his attitude. His maleness surrounded me. He, too, was cold and clinical. He seemed to take his frustrations about being awakened out on me. His demeanor made me feel more distrustful.

After some preliminary discussion about what had taken place, I was asked to undress. I found myself feeling very uncomfortable as I was undressing. I had not washed myself after the rape knowing it was important for the medical examination. I had such a strong feeling throughout these hours of wanting to take a long hot shower and cleanse myself of the rape. It was a fleeting thought.

During the examination, the doctor asked me questions which seemed out of his purview. Even though I knew it was necessary for the doctor to ask questions in order to know where to look for evidence, it was when he asked me if the rapist was "White or Colored?" that I felt violated again. Internally, I was outraged by this question. I classified him as a man with little awareness. My feelings of alienation grew. I responded by answering, "Which color are you referring to?" My response didn't sit too well with him. He seemed taken aback. My response was a way to vent some of my anger and hostility that I was now feeling not only about

14

the rape but about this man's attitude and behavior. I was glad (in some ways) that the rapist had been White so that the doctor's bias could not be confirmed—I thought about the political ramifications of his question. I wondered what were his assumptions about Black men or White men who raped. I was also pleased with myself for responding (although indirectly) to his statement. Even given the situation I was in, I was not going to allow this doctor to intimidate me nor let go of my strong feminist and anti-racist convictions.

He then asked me about my use of birth control. His eyebrows seemed to raise in a rather judgmental way when I told him I had an IUD. It seemed to me that he was questioning my being raped. After all, what was a single woman doing using an IUD? The doctor indicated that he had completed his part of the examination. He had not discussed the possibility of venereal disease so I asked him for penicillin as a prevention. Due to my distrust of the doctor and my own sense of danger, I wanted to make sure I didn't have to deal with the possibility of VD several weeks later. The physician then left the nurse to finish the examination. He instructed her to comb my pubic area and to check my fingernails in an effort to collect further evidence. I found myself reminding her to follow the procedures the doctor had given her. After three-and-one-half hours, I left the hospital physically and emotionally exhausted.

After standing in the hospital parking lot for a few minutes, I asked Jan to take me back to my apartment so that I could pick up some clothes, toiletries, and books for the next day. I stated that I would teach my 9:00 a.m. class. I was not going to let this incident change my life. I was going to be strong and control my own life. I was ready to continue with my life as if the rape had never occurred. Andrea confronted me by saying, "You can pretend that this never happened, you can go and teach tomorrow and deny it, but you will at some point have to deal with it. You've been raped and you need some time to put yourself and your

15

life back in order." Hearing that I was raped from someone else's mouth made me realize the seriousness of what had taken place. Her words made it clear that I had to take care of myself and attend to my needs. Heeding Andrea's advice, I decided not to teach the next day. Her confrontation served as an important reality check. I started to see the situation a bit more realistically. I had been raped—it would not go away—I would have to deal with the repercussions of the experience either now or later. I knew she was right.

We stopped briefly at my apartment. I was appalled to see everything covered with graphite left from the police's dusting for fingerprints. I looked around the apartment and felt estranged. What had been a very comfortable, warm and secure place several hours before was now very hostile and different. As I walked from room to room, I was shocked once more by the severity of the situation. I now noticed that the phone wires had been cut in both the kitchen and the study which I had not noticed before since I had called the police earlier from the bedroom phone. I felt even more unsafe and insecure. I concluded from the cut phone wires that the rapist must have had a knife. I realized that I really could have been killed. I then noticed that one of my photo albums in the study had been looked through and money had been taken from my wallet. I panicked when I realized that the rapist probably knew my name, who I was and where I worked. I also wondered how long he had been in my apartment before he had entered the bedroom. Why hadn't I heard him?

I looked for my cat, Bingo, but he was nowhere to be found. Apparently he ran away during the rape. He had made the journey with me from Massachusetts and had served as my companion and source of comfort for the past five years. I cried for my losses—my cat, my trust and my safety. So much had been taken from me in that twenty minutes. I felt overwhelmed with grief and sorrow. I felt that I had nothing left.

At Jan's house, Andrea and Jan sat with me while I

reacted to the last few hours. I was shaking, talking and crying all at the same time. It took several hours for me to
calm down. We then talked about how the situation should
be handled with other people. I adamantly stated that it
was fine for both Jan and Andrea to tell others. Politically,
I felt that rape should not be covered up or hidden. I gave
them permission to tell my colleagues and friends if they
chose to or if the situation arose. As dawn approached, we
decided to try and get some sleep. It had been a long and
arduous night.

I finally took that long-awaited shower. Somehow
when we got to Jan's house, my first need was to talk about
my feelings; the shower seemed less important. Now I looked
forward to sleeping but sleep was impossible. My thoughts
raced and flashes of the rapist with his hand over my mouth
permeated my mind. I tried sleeping in several different posi-
tions but the images kept on haunting me. After tossing and
turning for over an hour, I realized I was still too frightened
to sleep. I paced around the house for another hour and
finally sat down to write some of the feelings that were swelling within me. The following excerpt is an account of my
emotional state that morning:

> It's the morning after — I feel as if in a fan-
> tasy. Did this really happen to me? I just
> study about these things — Questions — I
> feel in touch with my vulnerability, my
> powerlessness, my anger. In a daze.

> Can I forget? Will I forget? Should I forget?
> I feel so confused. Continue as if it didn't
> happen — but it did!!!

> Feeling so alone in that hospital room. No
> one allowed to hold my hand. More men!!!
> My support just outside the door.

Anger — Anger at this system for allowing such maniacs to walk this earth. Anger at those two women next door — who couldn't, didn't warn me. Anger at that man — God-damn-son-of-a-bitch — for feeling he has the right to do what he pleases.

Anger at me — for not knowing better than to keep the windows open. For allowing myself to think I could be free in this country. For allowing myself the space I want, the room, for not being paranoid. For actually trusting. For not using my survival skills. Anger at me for thinking I was different!

Confused — Who to tell? What to tell them? Why do I want to tell them? What can others give me? What do I want from them? Support, love, concern. To share. I can't/won't hold this all inside of me — as my sole problem. It is a women's concern, issue. I need their love, comfort.

Rape has always been a painful thing. It is now a painful act/experience. Does one ever know what to do? Talk to him, analyze him, figure him out, ease his concerns, struggle, all the books in the world don't help.

Pumped up with penicillin. My ass hurts — My pride hurts. I feel wounded — conflicted. Loss — of part of me. Of Bingo, my cat, my friend, companion. It's a double mourning. For my own self and my cat.

Playing back the scene — it didn't happen — stop wishing — face it — it did! Do I have a home? Is this the kind of world I want to live in.

It — It — It, I can't even say rape! It's another denial.

Understanding how some women might want to forget about the rape at this point. Not to prosecute. Pushing it under the rug. It all makes sense.

Is this the end or just the beginning? Is this the stop or the start? Can I take that first step on the long journey back? I must!

As morning approached, I found myself calling several close friends in the East. Sharing with them my experience was a way to see if they would still accept me. In another way, it shifted some of my feelings of helplessness onto them. After all, what could they do being so far away? My rape, now, was a part of their reality as it was mine.

One of the most difficult decisions that I had to make at this time was whether or not to tell my friend, Richard, about the rape. Although I had left Massachusetts a month earlier, Richard and I still maintained an intimate relationship. We had shared almost two years of our lives together while I lived in Amherst. I finally decided to call but I was really unclear as to what I wanted from him. I found myself fearing his reaction. As I dialed the number, tears flooded my eyes and I started to lose my hard-won control and composure. When Richard answered the phone, I completely lost control of my emotions, and through my tears, I told him about the rape. He just listened for a long few minutes, but when he spoke, I knew that he was concerned and supportive. We talked for several more minutes. During this time, he told me that he still loved me and that he would be on the next plane out. I panicked. Part of me wanted him to be there to hold me but a stronger part of me didn't. I fought needing or wanting a man's protection. I wanted to make it by myself. I feared that if he came out that I would have to deal with him sexually. How would I respond? I told him that I would think about his coming out and would call him later that evening. I needed some time to consider this situation.

Throughout the day, I received much needed support. People that were aware of my experience called to see how or if they could help. Offers of concern and assistance were extended. One woman, Kris, accompanied me to the police station later that afternoon. Other women-friends stopped by to see me to make sure that I was all right. They shared their willingness to help. These women offered their understanding, their time and their love. I felt reassured. I also knew that they would be there if I needed them. I trusted their sincerity and willingness to help. Of all the women that stopped by to see me, four of them and I agreed to meet later on that same evening. Consequently, a support group coalesced.

Much of what we did that first evening was to help me decide about Richard's coming to Oklahoma. The group helped identify and clarify my major concerns. I decided, after weighing the pros and cons of the dilemma, to let him come out provided that he had no sexual expectations.

In my conversation with him that evening, I outlined my concerns. He agreed to come to Oklahoma under my conditions.

It was now less than twenty-four hours after the rape and my whole world had been drastically altered. Yet I continued on. I had survived the initial ordeal. My immediate needs had been met. I now felt a superficial sense of safety. I knew that there was support for me. It was time to pick up the shattered pieces of my life and put them in some order.

CHAPTER III

FEARS, PHOBIAS AND FANTASIES: PUTTING THE PIECES BACK TOGETHER

In the days that followed the rape, I made an attempt to reconstruct my life. Although I had given my friends permission to discuss the fact that I was raped, I found myself feeling apprehensive because I wasn't sure who knew about it. I did not know what to say to people or how to act around them. I wasn't sure whether to acknowledge the rape, assume that people were aware of my experience, or pretend as if nothing had occurred.

The University and local paper both contained accounts of the rape, which read: "A 26-year-old Oklahoma University Professor was raped in her East Side apartment last night." I was the only 26-year-old female professor at the university at that time. I imagined that all my colleagues and students had read the paper and, as I walked around campus, I felt very conspicuous and exposed. I had the feeling that everyone around me knew.

I was angry because the experience could not be kept separate from my work. I experienced a heightened sense of anxiety, too, because the police felt that the suspect could possibly be a student. Keeping this in mind, I looked suspiciously at every male student who might fit the description. I carefully watched their reactions and listened acutely

21

to their voices but none seemed to fit the image that remained in my mind.

During the next two weeks, my life seemed to return to some degree of normalcy. Richard came out from Massachusetts as we had planned. I continued teaching my classes as I had done before the rape. And I began to develop a much closer relationship with Andrea, Kris, Jan and Linda, all whom had served as a support base the night of my rape. I continued to live in the same apartment; I made sure that the windows and doors were always locked.

At the end of almost two weeks, I was feeling much stronger. I thought I had managed to successfully put the experience behind me. Richard's stay enabled me to feel secure and safe. He was very understanding and compassionate about the rape. What was particularly helpful was just his being there. He took all the cues from me and responded to my needs, not forcing his own. Richard returned to Massachusetts and I went off to California to teach for a week. I was curious to see what my reactions might be since this was the first time that I was alone since the rape. Again, I was determined not to let the rape experience affect me.

When I arrived in California, I was feeling a certain degree of assurance. However, when I checked into my motel, I made sure that there was a bolt lock on the door. In an effort to convince myself that I was unaffected by the experience, I decided to take a drive down Highway 1 from Monterey, where I was staying. I was clear that I was not going to allow the experience of the rape alter my behavior. As I was driving down High 1 near Big Sur, the car died. I pulled the car over and a man about my age stopped to help me. He offered to drive me to a service station. I jumped in the car with him and got help. Before the rape, I would not have done this; now I was attempting to prove that I was unaffected. Fortunately, the man was helpful but, in retrospect, I could have gotten killed. At this point, I was not seeing reality too clearly.

During the one week seminar, I found myself discussing my experience with a few select students. They were surprised that I was functioning so well given the newness of the experience. Their understanding reaffirmed my sense of internal strength. After class, I spent a few days with Ted, a therapist friend. I told him about the rape and was anxious to hear his response. We spent a good deal of time in those few days talking about my reactions. He, too, was surprised and pleased to see how well I was handling myself. He could not see, nor could I, any traumatic after-effects from the rape. In many ways I tried to convince myself that the rape had not affected me. In actuality, I was still denying that the rape actually occurred. By showing Ted, and myself, how well I was handling my reactions, I was able to hide from my real feelings. Little did I know this was only a lull in the storm to follow.

Upon returning to Norman, Oklahoma, I was hoping that my life would continue as it had been before the rape. I was still denying the reality of being raped but I did feel energized and stronger after my trip. My class had gone well, my visit with Ted was reaffirming and my confidence seemed restored.

When I returned to my apartment, I sensed that something was terribly wrong. I noticed immediately that the nightlight that I had left on was out. At first, I thought that it just burned out. I sensed in my gut, however, that it wasn't the reason. I didn't enter the apartment but went directly to the manager's office. She told me that another woman had been raped in the complex while I was away. I also found out that the same night the rape occurred, my apartment had been broken into again.

The police had found my front door open as they searched the complex grounds for the rapist the evening of the assault. The manager was not sure what, if anything, had been taken from my apartment. My false sense of security was once again shattered. I thought to myself—the rapist had returned. I was overwhelmed. My privacy and my life had been invaded again. I feared that the "rapist" was stalking my apartment awaiting my return.

I refused to go to the apartment alone. The manager's husband accompanied me. I even found myself distrusting him just because he was male.

The apartment appeared in order. I had imagined everything turned inside out. I started taking inventory of all my possessions. The only things missing were the TV and some jewelry which had sentimental value. I stayed long enough to collect my mail and a few books. I vowed never to return to live in that apartment again.

I ended up on Andrea's doorstep with my suitcase in hand and my sanity intact. She had offered me a place to stay immediately after the rape so I decided to take up her offer.

Reflecting back on the evening, I was thankful that I hadn't been home when the apartment was burglarized. The material losses seemed unimportant. I couldn't help but wonder what would have happened to me had I been alone in the apartment. I couldn't even imagine being raped a second time. All the defenses that I had so painstakingly constructed over the past month crumbled. Reality struck me. Once more, I felt terrified, vulnerable and defeated.

Journal Entry: October 1976:
"Feel unnerved. Don't like being so on edge.
Uncomfortable with myself. Violence again
in my life. Helpless, tired. God, am I tired."

I called the police the following day and reported the burglary. I also checked out which parts of town they considered safer to live. My support group and other friends helped me move into my new home. I turned the new house into a fortress. Every entrance was sealed. I put bolt locks on the doors and dowels in every window. I hoped that now I would be safe. I hoped that this would be the end to my feelings of fright and violence but it wasn't. It was just the beginning.

In the next few months, reactions to the rape began to surface. My behaviors, emotions and relationships were all being affected by the rape. Dealing with the rape became a daily part of my life. It overwhelmed me, consumed me and controlled my total being.

Journal Entry: November 1976:
"Want to withdraw. No place to go. No home. No place that's mine. Disoriented — Needy — Angered. Want to go home. Be loved. Be mothered, fathered. Can I make it? Feeling isolated, alone. Want to be held, touched, loved, need some security."

Although my new home was fortified with a multitude of locks, I rarely felt safe. I feared walking from my car to the well-lit front porch. I would imagine someone in the bushes would attack me before I could safely enter my home. Once inside, I immediately locked the front door. Still not feeling safe or secure, I then went on a ritualized room-to-room search. I put the lights on in every room, opened each and every closet and checked all the windows to insure that they were securely fastened. I checked behind the shower curtain to verify that there were no intruders.

Each time I went through this ritual, I felt ridiculous. I felt that I was being overly paranoid and yet I couldn't relax until I checked every part of the house. After completing the search and insuring that I was alone, I would finally feel some degree of safety.

I hated the night. I associated the rape experience with the darkness. When darkness approached, my fears escalated. Each evening I thought that perhaps this night would be different. Sleeping became a most difficult task. Often I would stay up as late as I could so that I would be exhausted and, hopefully, fall asleep. Other nights I would rely on a glass of wine to help ease my anxieties. However, these methods rarely worked.

I found that sleeping nude made me feel very uncomfortable so I started wearing a nightgown. I felt guilty and ashamed that I had been sleeping naked the night of the rape. Realistically, I knew that my not wearing a nightgown that night had little to do with what had happened. Emotionally, however, I felt a need to cover myself. I saw the nightgown serving as a thin protective shield.

I couldn't sleep while lying on my stomach. This was the position in which the rapist had found me. The problem was that I couldn't sleep in any other position either. When I would lie on my stomach, I would start having flashbacks to the rape. The memory was so vivid and real that I found it impossible to sleep. When I did doze, it would be a very shallow sleep. Noises such as the refrigerator clicking on, or the wind rustling through the trees would easily startle me awake. Often I would wake up thinking that someone was in the room. I would lie in bed terrified. My stomach would be knotted and my anxiety high—so high that I couldn't move even to turn the light on near my bed. As dawn approached, I would fall back to sleep for a few short hours of desperately needed rest.

As the months passed, I learned to systematically relax my mind and body in responses to noises. I could, at least, turn out the light or get out of my bed to make sure that all was in order. However, actually sleeping through a night took almost a year and a half.

I found myself reacting suspiciously to incidents which normally would have gone unnoticed. Anything out of the ordinary, I carefully watched. Strange cars and people all met with suspicion. One night stands out in my mind. I was asleep and the phone rang about 12:45 a.m. I immediately panicked. The man on the other end asked if the number he had reached was a pizza place. I told him that it wasn't and hung up. I was sure that it was the rapist checking to see if I was home. Although my phone number was unlisted, I was sure that he had tracked me down. I attempted to go back to sleep but my fears were too strong. Finally, I decided to look through the telephone book and checked every phone number until I found a pizza place with a number similar to mine. Once I verified that such a number existed, I was then assured that the call was an honest mistake.

During this period, I would only get sexually involved with a man if I was the one to initiate the contact. I desperately needed to feel in control around sexual contact. I also found myself getting sexually involved with a man partly as a way to feel protected. Having someone spend the night with me was one way to sleep at night. And yet, at the same time, I denied that the rape was affecting me. I denied my feelings and told no one of the terror and paranoia I was experiencing at night. I somehow didn't see the connection between my interaction with men and my inability to sleep.

I suppressed many of my feelings and negated others. I literally pushed them aside and hoped that over time they would dissipate. I put an enormous amount of time and energy into my work as an escape. I made an effort to appear strong, in control and capable of handling my life. In fact, many friends experienced me as being quite strong and capable of handling this crisis. By putting up an image of being strong, others around me knew little about the fearful and sleepless nights I would experience. By maintaining this facade, I kept myself from asking for help or allowing other people to see how desperately I needed them.

Although I had used my support group as a sounding board after the rape, I found myself, now, three months later, pulling away. My friends had done so much to help me. They had comforted me, listened to me and helped me move into my new home. I felt that I couldn't ask them for any more. I feared that they were tired of hearing about my experiences.

I sensed that too much of my time and energy was being spent worrying about the rape, my feelings and my analysis of my own reactions. I worried about infringing on my friends' time. I didn't want to bother them with my omnipresent problems. I was even getting tired of hearing

27

myself repeatedly replay the events of the rape. I thought that surely my friends had heard enough. At this point I did consider seeing a counselor as one way to sort through some of the feelings. I had sought a counselor's help in the past, when I completed my doctorate, as a way to enable me to get back in touch with my emotional side after dedicating four years of my life to the rigors of academic cognitive work, so I was not adverse to the counseling process. However, I found that there were no feminist counselors or therapists in the area. I had strong feelings about seeking help from people who do not hold feminist views. I was clear that since I was already blaming myself, I didn't need a therapist who would reinforce me in that area. I am also aware that part of me did not want to admit that I couldn't handle my reactions to the rape myself.

In addition to my fears of not wanting to infringe on my friends, I feared more deeply their rejection of me. In my effort to be strong, I told myself that I was not responsible for what happened to me. I couldn't accept the myth that, "Women ask for it." I didn't feel that, "A woman couldn't be raped unless she allowed herself to be raped." Emotionally, however, I had internalized feelings of shame, guilt and responsibility. I wondered continuously what I could have done to avoid the rape. I perceived this as a "feminist dilemma."

How could I, as a feminist, actually feel guilt or shame about the rape? I knew my feelings were incongruent with what I believed about rape but I still continued to conflict internally. I wasn't just holding in a tremendous amount of pain, I was desperately trying to maintain an image for myself and my friends. I was afraid to share these feelings for fear that I would lose some of their respect for me as a feminist.

I did continue to talk to individuals in my support group about many other aspects of the rape. However, the focus of my conversation was usually on past feelings and rarely did I dwell on the present. It was easier to discuss my feelings of the previous month rather than the turmoil I was now experiencing.

Repeatedly, I would discuss the events of the rape itself and the ordeal at the hospital. Consequently, I would only deal with those aspects of the rape that were relatively easy for me to address. The deeper feelings of shame, guilt, disgust and anger I didn't want to discuss in any depth.

One day, about three months after the rape, I stayed home because I felt like I was losing control. My facade of being strong was slowly shattering. My mind swirled and my body trembled. I didn't know what was happening to me. I perceived my being a feminist as the source of my power, control and intelligence. I saw myself as being strong, capable and independent. I feared finding out that I was not as strong as I thought I was. This reflection was the cement that was holding me together. If my self-perception was, in fact, inaccurate, what would I have left to hold onto?

This later feeling of vulnerability, of losing my mind, was yet another level of the violence of the rape. The rape was a violation of the body and the spirit. In short, I now feared two kinds of death.

Journal Entry: December 1976:
I'm feeling so out of control. So depressed.
My fears, my paranoia are overwhelming me.
I can't focus. Run away— Be strong. I'm
caught. Uptight.

Scared— OH, GOD, am I scared. I feel so
vulnerable again. How much can I take?
How can I keep on going? I just can't. . .
can't.

Friends — don't know what to do. I don't
know what I need. Help! Alone.

Anger— Tears once again. Why me? Realization of my unknowing. Some are always victims. Can I ask for help? Will I ever stop fearing? Should I leave? Stay? What route to take? Too much for me to deal with.

I'm being torn apart. Inside out. Ripping away layer after layer. Coat after coat. Defenses lost — Strength to battle is being extinguished. Dying a slow—slow death inside. No energy to move. No energy to think. No energy to cope. No energy to work. I'm losing control.

TOO TIRED—but can't stop.

At the same time that I was experiencing this turmoil, my support group members were experiencing a dilemma, too. They could see that I was struggling with my emotions. They observed and sensed that I was having strong reactions to the rape — reactions which weren't being expressed. In our conversations, they listened not only to what I was saying but also to what I wasn't saying. They were sensitive to those aspects of the rape over which I would lightly pass, joke about, or never discuss. On one hand, they respected my ability to let them know when I was ready to address particular issues which bothered me. They were also reluctant to pry and somewhat hesitant to push certain topics. As a result, a stalemate occurred. I needed desperately to talk about my deep feelings but I was reluctant to talk to them. They had given me so much of their time and compassion. I didn't want them to feel used. How could I ask them for more? I was reluctant to ask and they were willing to help but hesitant to push me.

This stalemate was finally broken when Kris made it a point to say that if I wanted to talk, she was willing and available. She acknowledged that even though it was three months after the rape, she assumed I still had many unresolved feelings. At first I refused the offer. I told her that I was doing fine. The following day, I reconsidered. I asked her to come over and spend an afternoon with me. This particular afternoon was a critical part in the healing process. Over a bottle of wine, I poured out my feelings about the conflicts which raged within me. Kris shared some of her own feelings of helplessness. At times, she could see that I was in pain and struggling with my emotions but she didn't know how to respond. She feared pushing me too far.

Our conversation served to end the stalemate. I no longer felt so alone or alienated. I knew I could rely on Kris. We agreed that she would let me know when she did feel like she had heard enough. This enabled me to feel like I didn't have to hold back my feelings. I trusted her honesty.

With a solid base reestablished, I began to share with her the deep and varied emotions which were causing me such pain. Kris served as a good listener, a clarifier and a friend. She also honestly shared her own reactions to my situation. This made it easier for me to talk about the deep conflicts I was experiencing.

Kris helped me understand my feminist dilemma. For all of my life, I had internalized the myths about women's responsibility in rape. How could I expect myself not to hold those anachronistic attitudes and feelings? My relatively new awareness and new consciousness of rape contradicted all the old stereotyped attitudes that I had emotionally internalized.

Kris had given me unconditional compassion for my feelings. She did not, as I had feared, reject me or negate the emotions I was experiencing. In fact, through our conversation I became clearer that I used that as an excuse not to face the feelings and conflicts I was experiencing. She helped me examine my situation. I began to talk about other emotions more specifically. I disclosed the reasons for feeling shame and guilt. I verbalized in more detail about how disgusted and humiliated I had felt during the assault. I was able to shed some of those feelings by sharing them. We also talked about my present behavior, such as my ritualized searches, my not sleeping and my paranoia that the rapist was still out to get me. I thought that Kris would clearly say that I was crazy and suggest that I needed psychological care. Instead she lent her understanding. She made it clear that my reactions were normal reactions to a very life-threatening situation. It was apparent to me that our discussion served as a catharsis. Kris had broken the stalemate. I now knew that I still had a right to continue asking my support group friends for help. I also realized that I was not going crazy and that what I was experiencing was a normal reaction to the assault. I felt less alienated and less alone as a result of our being together. I was relieved. I had somewhere to turn for help. In overcoming this stalemate, I was ready to take the next step in the healing process.

CHAPTER IV

FRIENDS AND FAMILY:
THE IMPACT OF RAPE
ON SIGNIFICANT OTHERS

Although I felt tremendously isolated and alone after the rape, I was certain of one thing. I knew that I would need the understanding and assistance of my friends and my family to help in the process of healing which was to follow.

One decision which I was faced with immediately following the rape was who to tell about my experience. I was never the kind of woman who would remain silent about events in my life. Rather, I was usually open about my experiences and the emotions associated with it. Talking about myself was a way to gain a better insight into my feelings and, in turn, gain clarity on what issues were germane at that moment. It was a way to collect information from others and, at the same time, plan a course of action. This was a familiar process for me so I felt that I needed to use this same method in dealing with my rape experience.

Days after the rape, I found myself calling friends in Norman and old friends from the east coast for help. My rationale was that if they were truly friends, they would be able to help in some way. Somehow I hoped that by sharing my pain with them , my emotional struggle would be eased. I also felt that it was important not to keep this experience hidden. After all, I wasn't at fault for what had happened but I still needed reassurance that my friends, both male and female, would still accept me. If they could accept the reality of rape and its effects on me, then there was a chance that I could do the same.

I found it almost impossible to remain silent. There was a sense of relief when I described the experience to others because, often, they too would share my feelings of helplessness. Rape had now touched their lives as well as mine. They had to sort through their own responses and feelings about rape and, more specifically, my experience.

I found my friends reacting in various ways. Some responses I had anticipated while others I had not. Although not consciously aware of it at the time, I internalized their responses toward me as a basis for deciding which friendships I would maintain and which friendships I would pull away from.

I tested the reactions of each person I encountered or called. The initial responses to my experience was a clue as to whether I could count on that person to be helpful or not. Some individuals would share their concern for my immediate safety and would ask specific questions about the rape and my reactions. Other friends would reassure me that they were available if I needed them.

The friends with whom I drew closer demonstrated a congruency between their words and their actions. They not only told me they were there but showed it. They shared not only their feelings of concern for me but were also willing to discuss their own reactions of shock, disbelief and anger. I reacted more favorably to those people who were honest enough to share their own feelings. I drew closer to them because of our ability to share our emotions. I received their attention and understanding on a deep level.

As time passed, I grew closer to individuals who followed up on their initial statements. Letters and telephone calls which I received after the rape reconfirmed their understanding of my experience and their concern about my reactions to it.

One friend in particular had a strong impact on my ability to work through the trauma I was experiencing after the rape. Nancy, a friend of mine from the University of Massachusetts, was the only woman I had known who had been raped. I thought of all my friends that she would best understand what I was experiencing. I called her shortly after the rape and talked to her about what had happened. She wrote a letter a few days later filled with her compassionate response. Her letter gave me license to reexamine my own suffering. Her words enabled me to recognize that I was not alone in this struggle. Being able to read her statements and know that she knew what I had experienced was a powerful way to encourage me not to repress my own feelings. Her letter read:

> Judy,
>
> I was so shaken by your crisis. I wish with all my heart that you hadn't gone through that and that you didn't have to have the miserable knowledge of this particularly horrifying brutality, emotional even more than physical. Be awfully good to yourself; awfully tolerant of unexpected reactions; and ask for what you need even if that seems weird — like being left alone but with the safety of someone else in a nearby room.
>
> And don't be ashamed of anything you did that resulted in your being alive and physically 'in one piece' as you put it. I used every counseling skill I had and it still took two hours to get him out — and for awhile, I felt guilty about that, as if I'd been unfairly manipulative. You may not go through that (I hope not), but don't be surprised or too upset if you feel flashes of shame. You were forced to do the most

abhorrent thing for a sensitive woman to whom sex is a rich, sweet, deep part of a real relationship. And you'll inevitably go through incredible changes — anger, fierce anger, mourning, sorrow, bewilderment.

I'm so sorry, so sorry, but I trust you to respect yourself in every way.

Love to you
dear Judy—
Nancy

In addition to support, Nancy's letter had yet another effect on me. I recalled how little I had done to help her when she was raped. After receiving her letter, I remembered how difficult it was for me to relate to her experience at the time. I didn't reach out or even inquire over time how I could give her what she needed. I always felt that she was a strong and independent woman. I also thought that she could handle this crisis. I realized, after reading her letter, how I had contributed to keeping her stereotyped as "being strong." I had not reached out or allowed her to share her fears or feelings in the months after her experience of being raped. I recalled our discussing her experience only once immediately following the assault. I felt so helpless at the time I didn't know what to do. I was afraid to pry. I told her I was there if she needed me, yet I had been puzzled by her seeming avoidance of the issue several months later. Now, after my own experience, I realized how very difficult it must have been for her to ask for help. I felt some guilt for having let her down when she needed me. I felt selfish for calling on her for support now when I had been unable to giver her mine. I began to see with some clarity the struggle which my other friends were experiencing in their attempts to help me. It was a painful but valuable insight. I realized that I would have to find ways to make it easier for them to help me.

As I disclosed my experience of being raped, I began to discover other disturbing information. I slowly learned about how many of my close friends had also been raped at some time in their lives. The sharing of my experience enabled them to be more open to sharing their experiences with me. Those women who had been raped understood my feelings of fear, shame, guilt, anger, helplessness, alienation and loneliness. For some, it was the first time they had shared their feelings with anyone else. For many it had been kept within as a deep, dark secret.

A close friend revealed that she had been repeatedly raped by her father when she was younger. Though the incidents had occurred more than fifteen years ago, she had never discussed it with anyone. Another close friend had been raped by an employer when she was a teenager; another by her boyfriend's roommate while she was in college. They had all remained silent until now. My experience had surfaced these well-hidden parts of their lives, forcing them to confront their own feelings and to face their repressed emotions.

The healing journey was not for me alone. The sharing of my experience was instrumental in unlocking the tribulations which other women had encountered. For some, having opened up "Pandora's Box" forced them to begin reevaluating their own experiences. As a result, some of these women drew closer to me, serving as a support group of survivors; while others withdrew, not wanting to face the rekindled feelings surrounding their own assaults.

I was overwhelmed by the fact that women I had known so well had never shared this part of themselves with me. I learned slowly and painfully just how many women did have personal encounters with rape. Together, we mourned our losses.

On the other hand, when I shared my experience with other friends, instead of support I would often receive a response of avoidance or denial. This would take the form of a statement such as, "At least you're all right and survived."

No follow-up questions were asked. No sharing of their own feelings occurred. Different friends would assume that I was managing all right and would superficially note that it seemed as if I were getting my life back to normal. Yet there was no checking as to whether their assumption was accurate. What appeared to be statements of concern had no backbone. They were superficial responses lacking both depth and caring. From there, people would often change the subject. It was clear to me that they did not want to hear about my experience. It seemed that rape was too threatening a topic for them to discuss. These individuals displayed a clear uneasiness with the subject. I believe that this reaction when demonstrated by women was often the result of their own fears of being raped. If they acknowledged and dealt with the reality of my being raped, they would also have to acknowledge and examine rape as a reality in their own lives. It was an incredibly threatening and frightening thought. I believe that my experience made some of my women friends get in touch with their own vulnerability because they may not have wanted to own this part of reality. They denied my experience instead.

Other reactions to my experience came in the form of giving advice. One male friend told me the best thing I could do was to forget about the experience — put it aside and go on living. This kind of response showed me his lack of understanding and compassion. It was obvious to me that he had a difficult time relating to the terror of being raped. There was a chasm in his ability to comprehend feelings of helplessness and terror. After all, I had not been physically abused; therefore, his attitude was, "It's over. Just pretend it was a bad dream." Although many times I wanted to just forget about it, this was not possible. One other suggestion was that I purchase a handgun. I didn't see this as being helpful either. As a matter of fact, I viewed this suggestion as a classic projection on the part of the person who suggested it.

One painful response came from a dear male friend

with whom I had worked while in graduate school. He was a professional counselor and human relations expert. After relating my experience to him, he replied, "I know you're strong and can handle it. I just hope you're not like some of those women who carry this thing around forever." This response served to alienate me from him. I realized that his response put boundaries around the kind of things I could now share with him. It became clear to me that I did not have the freedom to tell him when I didn't feel so strong or could not handle my responses. I no longer trusted him in quite the same way as I did before the rape.

I perceived a clear difference in the way men and women responded to my rape experience. Some men had internalized the myths of rape so deeply that they associated rape as a sexual experience. They wondered why I was so upset. Other men would make jokes about wishing a woman would rape them. Once again, this demonstrated to me a lack of sensitivity and understanding. As part of the internalization of the myths of rape, I felt that they put the blame on me. Questions such as, "Had I tried to fight?", "Was I sure the rapist had a weapon?", "Why had I left the window open?", only made me feel more distanced from them. The more "macho" men would become indignant and deal with the issues as only they could. They offered their protection. They offered to kill the rapist if they could get their hands on him. Although I often had that same thought, I viewed their response as coming more from their own ego needs or ways of handling a physical violation rather than for me. They never followed up and asked me how they could help — rather, they assumed they knew. The concern for them was how they were going to handle their feelings, not how to help me with mine.

One of the most difficult decisions I had to make was whether to tell my family about the rape. I decided that I would tell them, but not until I returned to New York. I was going home for winter break so I waited until then. I reasoned that my parents were just getting used to the idea that I was independent and able to manage on my own. My parents were somewhat overprotective. My move to Oklahoma had been met with their disapproval.

It wasn't until I was twenty-two that I left home for the first time to attend graduate school. In fact, I was the only person in my family to move outside of New York. My parents had hoped that when I completed my doctoral degree that I would find a job in the New York City area. They resented my moving fifteen hundred miles away from home.

I assumed that if I told my parents about the rape, they would immediately fly to Oklahoma and attempt to convince me to move back to New York. I needed their support but not their overprotection. I also needed to know that I could survive the rape experience without their intervention. I needed some time to deal with my own feelings before dealing with theirs. It would also give them a chance to see that I was, in fact, doing well and able to handle myself.

Part of my reluctance to tell them about my experience was based on my assumptions about how they would respond. I assumed that they would not offer understanding but rather make me feel more guilty. I imagined them blaming me for leaving my window open; for not taking my mother's advice about getting a second floor apartment; and, most important, for moving out to Oklahoma against their better judgment. I was already aware of each of these dimensions. I didn't need or want to hear those arguments from them, particularly because I felt that they were partially correct.

Several days after I was raped, my parents called. My mother expressed great concern. She stated that she felt something was wrong. She repeatedly asked if I was all right. I chose not to tell her about the rape. It was uncanny that she knew something was wrong but didn't know precisely what.

Several weeks later, when my apartment had been burglarized, I told them about the burglary incident. They

40

call repeatedly urging me to move back to New York. From their reaction, I was reassured that I had made the right decision in not telling them about the rape.

Before leaving Oklahoma for winter break, I spent some time with my support group in an attempt to find ways to tell my parents about being raped. I was extremely anxious about going home. I wanted my parents love and support but not their criticism. I felt strongly about their knowing about the rape because it was such a critical experience in my life. I knew that if I did not tell them, it would create a gap in our relationship. I didn't want to keep it from them. I knew, too, that my parents were sensitive to my feelings. They would know something was wrong just by being with me. Yet, I still feared that they would make me feel guilty, blame me and ultimately blame themselves. My support group helped me identify ways to tell my parents.

One method which we came up with to deal with my parents was to form boundaries for their reactions. I imagined all the possible responses which they might have. I prepared myself for their varied reactions. My attempt was to maintain control of the situation and of myself. I, therefore, decided to be as honest with them as I could and share with them first my reason for not telling them sooner. I would outline what I needed from them and what I didn't need. In this way, I maintained my control and my power.

When I arrived in New York, my parents were waiting at the airport. They expressed their curiosity about Oklahoma, my job and my new friends. My mother was also curious about why I had suddenly moved from my apartment when it was burglarized. I felt extremely uncomfortable and changed the subject. I decided that the airport was definitely an inappropriate place to discuss what had actually happened in Oklahoma.

At the dinner table that evening, I told my parents that I had not explained everything about the burglary. I related that I wanted to tell them face-to-face so they could see that I was all right. I made it clear why I wanted to tell them

41

and what I needed from them. I also stressed that I did not want them to feel that they had to rescue me. Making every effort to appear calm and in control of myself, I told them what had happened. I made a successful effort not to cry. I tried not to let my parents know how emotionally upsetting the experience was for me.

My mother extended her support. She shared her feelings of disbelief that such an event could happen to me. She shared that she had intuitively known that something was very wrong. She was utterly shaken. We discussed her phone call of several months earlier which occurred right after the rape. She also stated that she had been curious as to why I had moved so suddenly when my apartment had been burglarized. When she learned that a rape occurred in the apartment complex the night of the burglary and of my own experience, the entire scene fell into place. She did not ask a lot of questions nor did she ask how she could be of any assistance to me. She did, however, express her anger towards me for not telling her at the time. She felt rejected. It was apparent at the end of the conversation that her emotional state was in turmoil.

My father was also in shock. As a father and as a man, he felt that he had let his "little girl" down. He felt that he had somehow failed because he could not protect me. It was apparent that my experience was uncomfortable for him to address. My father is a very sensitive man. However, it is often difficult for him to acknowledge his emotions and reactions. At the dinner table, he sat and listened silently. His anxiety was extremely high.

Later that evening, we were talking in the kitchen. He was aware that he had made little contribution at the dinner table. He said, "Well, you know what they say about rape. If you are going to get raped, you might as well lay back and enjoy it." I was shocked and completely crushed by his statement. I couldn't believe that my father could be so insensitive—so brutal. It was hard to believe that he would make a joke about something so serious. I was incensed. I did, however, recognize that it was his discomfort with the fact that his daughter had been violated and brutalized—yet, I felt so much anger at him for even making the statement. It was as though he had no idea of what rape was all about or what I was feeling. He, too, was a victim of all the internalized myths concerning rape.

My sadness overwhelmed me. My own father was unable to lend support or to share his feelings directly with me. I felt alienated from him. I attempted to make light of his remark by recognizing it as his inability to cope with my situation but the hurt ran deep and created a rift in our relationship. Although he was my father, I classified him as an oppressive male. Whereas before I saw my father as someone who was sensitive to my needs, I now felt a great deal of mistrust. Over the years, he had been an encourager in my career efforts but now I felt distanced. I mourned the loss of our relationship. I didn't feel that I could even share with him how much his statement had affected me. I withdrew from him with his words branded in my thoughts. I wondered—if my father was unable to understand my situation and be there when I needed him—could any other man?

Although compassionate at first, my mother was also having a difficult time dealing with the reality of my being raped. The next day on our way to visit my aunt, she said, "I'm glad you're okay, but we don't have to mention this to any of the relatives." The underlying message was very clear. My mother didn't want to deal with my experience. She felt shame and responsibility for the fact that I was raped. My mother had also felt some guilt for not protecting me from what had happened. She saw my rape as a reflection on her as a mother. She felt, as my father did, as a failure. She anticipated that if I told my relatives they would blame her for allowing me to move to Oklahoma. She didn't want to hear that from them. Although I understood why she felt as she did, I too felt blamed. The message I heard was that I was the criminal, not the victim. My mother wanted to shelter this experience from the family and I wanted them to know. Once again, my power was taken away from me. I had no rights and what was worse, I felt at fault for bringing this bad news into the family and creating a crisis.

My mother had told my brother about what had happened. Here again, my power was usurped. I didn't even get the opportunity to tell him directly. His reaction was that he wanted to get a gun and kill the guy for me. Although it was his way to let me know he was angry about the situation, he never asked me what I needed or how he could help me. This response wasn't helpful to me at all.

The rape was not mentioned again during my ten day stay. I felt relieved by having told my family. But their response left me feeling lonely, uncared for and more distanced. I had hoped that their reactions would be different. I had hoped because we were family that they would be able to give the kind of support that no one else could. I had hoped that they would be able to fix things and make them better. Nothing had changed, yet everything was different.

However, what I was unaware of at the time was what effect my being raped had on my parents. While I interpreted their responses as a lack of understanding and a lack of compassion on their part, in reality, their responses were very deep and personal. Later I was to find out by talking with my mother that she had sought out her own support group to help her deal with her feelings about my being attacked and her own inability to know what to do. She needed a place to now deal with her pain. Similarly, my father spent many hours of self-reflection feeling helpless and as a failure to me. My parents spent a good deal of time and energy in the months after my visit sorting through their own reactions of anger, feeling helpless and blaming themselves for what had occurred to me. In many ways, their reactions were similar to mine.

I left New York realizing that no one could make my feelings change or vanish. I also realized that even my parents, who had raised and known me for twenty-six years, couldn't make me feel better or know what to do about my situation. I was disappointed and, for the first time, realized just how alone I was in the world. I recognized that the healing process was for me to work through by myself; others could lend understanding, compassion and an open ear, but I would have to struggle through the experience by myself. No one could take away the pain.

The Rape Victim As Man Hater, or They All Hate Men: Don't They?

A stereotypic portrayal of women who have been raped is that of "Man-Hater." Much of the media shows that once a woman has been raped, she becomes overly hostile to all men. Cognitively, I made a decision that I would not play out that role. Although politically I feel that all men are potential rapists in that our society supports violence by men against women, I did not want to blame all men for my situation. Intellectually, I knew that I was raped by only one man. I attempted to make it a point not to fear or hate all men. However, my interactions with men were clearly affected by my experience.

I did a great deal of testing of the men I would meet by telling them about my being raped. I would await their response. Their response was an indicator about whether or not I would deal with them any further. If a man indicated some degree of concern, honesty and understanding, I would identify him as a person with whom I could get involved. If his response was to make a joke or a derogatory statement, or to avoid the subject, I immediately decided to have little more to do with him. These types of comments often led to arguments and, consequently, I would become hostile and angry.

A second test in my encounters with men took place around sexuality. I found myself being the initiator in all sexual encounters. I needed the security and control of the situation. If I was attracted to a man, I would pursue him.

If he pursued me, I would back off. This control dynamic was essential on my part. I also found myself maintaining emotional distance in my relationships with men. Because so much of my energy was tied up in trying to deal with the aftermath of the rape, it was difficult to get emotionally involved. On a different level, however, this response was in reaction to my fearing men in general. I was extremely vulnerable as a result of the rape. I didn't want to be hurt by a man again. I, therefore, would only allow myself to care for someone to a certain point. Then, once I reached that point, I would cut off my feelings or terminate the relationship.

In retrospect, I believe that another response to the rape was to subtly exploit men that I would meet. During the rape, something precious had been taken from me. Sex had been made meaningless. I was made to feel like an object and, as a reaction to that dehumanization, I made my sexual encounters meaningless, too.

Several months after the rape, I found myself sleeping with several different men. The intimacy of the sexual encounter which I had so much enjoyed before was gone. This behavior was my way of exploiting men and a way to deal with my anger and hostility. It was a subtle way of regaining lost control and of having power over men. At the time, I viewed my behavior as a way to prove to myself that the rape had not affected me but my behavior was clearly an overreaction to all that was happening.

Finally, sleeping with different men was one way of gaining some protection. It was one way that I was able to sleep through the night and feel safe.

The issue of protection was a constant internal battle with me. About a year after the rape, I met a man and began a relationship which culminated in our living together. I fought that decision for a while feeling that I still needed to prove to myself that I could live alone. On one hand, I felt that I was ready for a meaningful relationship. But the rape experience was still very much a part of me even one year later. Initially, my partner was understanding of my reactions to the rape, but as time passed he appeared to resent me for having been raped. My experience was affecting his lifestyle, too. He felt that it was intruding upon his life and was angry about it. It was too much for him to handle. Even though I felt safer with him around, I needed the security of bolt locks on the doors. I still felt terrorized at night when I heard noises so I would sleep with all the windows closed. He began to question my sincerity in the feelings I maintained concerning the experience. He saw my reactions of fear as a way of holding onto the banner of being a "rape victim." The more he shared his resentment and anger, the more distant we became. What was particularly alienating and humiliating was his sharing his feelings publicly. It was at this point that I emotionally began to terminate the relationship. The physical separation followed a few months later.

In retrospect, this relationship was based in part on a real need for me to feel some safety and protection in my life. At the time I could not admit this to myself for fear of not being as strong or in control of my reactions as I would like to think of myself.

It appears that I had categorized people according to their response to my experience. Individuals reacted to me based on their own assumptions, feelings and experience with rape. It was apparent that there was a continuum of responses ranging from those that were deterimental to me and to our relationship, to responses that were helpful in enabling me to address the reactions I was having as a result of the rape.

The first level of response which I label as being most unhelpful came from individuals who were unable and uncomfortable dealing with rape as a reality. From men, the response might be to tell a joke about rape. Women would often ask questions like, "Why did you leave the window open?" The main element at this level of response was to deny the reality of rape. By denying my being raped, these women could deny that they, too, were potential victims. These individuals clearly had internalized myths about rape—

such as: a woman can only be raped if she chooses to be; that rape is a sexual act; or that somehow she can do something to avoid it. Other individuals at this level would express a desire to kill the rapist. These individuals were responding to their own internalized myths; their own fears about rape; and their own needs at the moment. This kind of response alienated me from the individual. It was obvious that they could not help me in any way.

The second level of response came from individuals who would attempt to console me but were helpless because of their lack of skills and knowledge concerning my feelings. Often, individuals at this stage displayed a great deal of comfort when dealing with the fact that I had been raped. They would share initial statements of regret but their actions would limit any follow up. They subtly indicated a desire not to hear more about the experience. By changing the subject or by telling me how strong I was, they limited what I could discuss with them. Individuals, at this stage, did well giving advice but made little attempt at understanding my feelings, needs or reactions to the rape.

A third level of response came from individuals who were able to share their own feelings about the incident. They would make empathetic statements upon hearing of the rape. They were willing to risk asking about other aspects of the rape without feeling that they would offend me. These types of responses allowed me to see that person as a potential support system. In the interchange, I would feel heard and know that I was cared for and accepted.

The fourth level of response was the most helpful to me, both immediately following the rape and in the months afterward. These individuals were able to find out what I needed and to ask me how they could help meet those needs. Once those needs were identified they were able to help me help myself. These individuals were also able to share their own honest reactions and feelings about my situation. Therefore, someone might share that they feel so outraged that they wanted to kill the rapist but this reaction would be coupled with identifying what I needed from them and how I was feeling. In addition, friends at this level did not respond to me only when I addressed the rape but, rather, they would take the initiative and check periodically to see how I was doing. I felt that I could more easily discuss my feelings with them and be accepted without recrimination. I felt a genuine interest and concern from them. The women in my support group clearly demonstrated this level of response.

Just as I was reacting to different responses from different individuals, my friends and family were also trying to make sense of the turmoil. My being raped now made rape a reality in their lives, too. In many ways they felt victimized.

The major emotion which most friends and family members reported was an overwhelming sense of helplessness. The confusion they experienced existed between being aware of my struggle and not knowing how to react to it.

One of my male students shared his thoughts and reactions to my assault in the following letter. Although the letter was written four years after the rape, it demonstrates the intense struggle of the person standing outside watching the victim suffer and, yet, unable to cross over and render help.

A letter from Tom: 9/30/79:

I heard about the rape that night or very early the next morning. Jan telephoned me as I recall and was very upset. At the time, the thought went through my mind, 'What can I do?' I never came up with an answer. I still haven't. Perhaps this letter is all I can do now. I remember wanting to do so much—sit with you, hug you, cry with you, help you secure your apartment, help you move to your new house, cook you a meal. . .millions of things. I wanted so much to be warm, caring, understanding and hearing. BUT, it seemed that you had all of those needs accomplished with Kris, Andrea, Jan and Linda. I felt fairly useless in the area of support. Mainly because I was a male and you were raped by a male. How would you have related to me if I did reach out? I wasn't sure then, nor am I sure yet. Further, you were/are perceived by me to be a very strong, independent, self-sufficient person. How could I help? Also, entering my mind was the knowledge of your being such a strong feminist. This coupled with my male chauvinist guilt feelings made me feel even more guilty about the rape. In others words, here I am a semi-enlightened MCP who tries (although not too well) to recognize injustice towards females and to look for places to correct wrongs and feelings that— well, shit, I'm a male and women are being shit upon by males; therefore, I must be awful (a) not to do anything, and (b) to be a male. Rational or not is not the issue. Reality is the issue and I felt guilty—personal guilt for the male 49% of the human species. And, your rape only served to deepen and broaden that guilt. I was a member of the part of the species who did that??? I could not handle it either mentally or interpersonally—so, I did nothing until now. And, this isn't much. So, your rape served to widen the gap that I feel exists between males and females in general.

It appears that I made it easier for some people to come closer than others. Those people that I relied upon for help have discussed with me how strongly my experience touched their lives. Many of the women had to think about rape for the first time as a reality in their own lives. Questions about how they might react in such a situation became paramount. Furthermore, the reality of not being safe even in a small town like Norman, Oklahoma, became a new awareness for many. Securing homes, locking cars and taking precautions became new behaviors in their lives.

For others, my being raped brought back painful hidden memories of repressed experiences. These newly opened doors had to be addressed for them, too. For my parents the experience made them feel as if they failed to protect me from the cruelties of the world. For some of my male friends was the fear of my hating them for what another man had done. For my partner it was the constant intrusion of the rapist in our lives even a year after the assault. Each person had to face their reactions to me and to my being a victim of sexual assault. Thus, in many ways, we were all victimized by the rape.

CHAPTER V

TO TESTIFY OR NOT TO TESTIFY

A serious dilemma facing many rape victims is whether or not to go to trial if the rapist is apprehended. The thought of testifying brings to mind the horror of replaying the rape in intimate detail in front of twelve unknown jurors. I experienced the same sense of fear.

As a feminist, I had felt that if I were ever raped I would definitely press charges and go to court. I had a difficult time understanding why women would refuse to identify a known rapist and I had often condemned those women. Politically, I felt that it was critical to press charges and go through with the trial so that the rapist would be stopped and put behind bars. I viewed this aspect of the process as a critical way to protect not only the woman who had been raped but all women. When a woman refuses to identify a suspect or press charges, the man learns that raping will not be punished; he is allowed to go free. For all these reasons I could not understand why a woman would not be willing to report the rape, identify a suspect, press charges, or be willing to serve as a witness for the state with her testimony. It was only when faced with the reality of this situation did I understand the difficulty of such a choice. My attitudes and beliefs concerning the judicial process were being tested.

Six weeks after the rape, the police still did not have a

suspect. The descriptive information I had given the police was incomplete, because I couldn't describe his face. I remembered such things as the man's size, body type, hair color and voice pattern but it apparently wasn't enough for the police to go on. I also wondered how much of an effort had been made to try and find the rapist. After all, I wasn't the only woman who had been raped in that apartment complex. Although the detective on the case kept me informed of his progress, I had little hope that he would find a suspect or that I would even be able to identify the man if he did.

One night, to my surprise, the detective called and said that they had apprehended a potential suspect. He asked if I would be willing to make an identification. I told him that I would definitely be available. The only problem that still needed to be worked out was some jurisdictional issues between two counties as the man was found in a different county. The detective stated that he would get back to me and let me know if and when I was needed for the identification. I hung up the phone and experienced a myriad of emotions. My immediate response was fear. I did not want to face the man—I feared even being near him. I also began to imagine the courtroom scenario. I reran each moment of the rape through my mind. I saw the attorney for the defendant twisting my response to indicate I had been an accomplice—that I had not protested. I saw myself on the witness stand being cross-examined, being blamed and being discredited for not being a virgin, for being a single woman and a feminist. I could hear the attorney asking me why had I left my window open? Why had I slept naked? Why had I encouraged the man by telling him he was okay? Was, in fact, this a case of rape? I also imagined my past sexual experiences being distorted to the rapist's advantage. I wondered if Oklahoma was a state that allowed such information at the trial. I was overwhelmed with emotion. I just wanted the experience to be over.

For the first ime in my life, I understood why women

chose not to testify. I could clearly understand their fears, their pain, their anguish and their guilt. It was extremely difficult to admit this new awareness. I was caught between feelings of revenge, doing what I knew had to be done and feelings of wanting to forget the rape and take no action in an effort to try and leave it all behind me. Part of me hoped that if I did not identify the man and press charges, somehow my reactions to the rape would go away. However, deep down inside, I knew this was not the case. I could not run away from the reality of what had occurred. I knew I would have to go ahead with court proceedings if necessary. It was one way to use my power to help other women and revenge my situation. Unfortunately, I never got the opportunity to act on this resolve. The detective called back several days later stating that there had been an error and they did not have a suspect for identification. Although I felt temporarily relieved by the phone call, I also experienced a great deal of anger that the man was not caught. Later that day I was to experience fear, too, realizing that the rapist was still at large. To my knowledge, he has still not been caught.

Personally, I have not faced the trial situation but because of the work that I do, I am in constant communication with women who have gone through the trial experience. A friend and colleague of mine, Rosalie Taylor, has been actively involved in the trial process in the Oklahoma City area. Rosalie was one of the founders of the Oklahoma City Women's Center. She began a rape crisis line and trained as an advocate for rape victims.

A rape advocate is a person who serves as an intermediary for the victim. The advocate is specially trained to provide information to the woman who has been raped about medical and legal procedures. The advocate also provides support and assists the victim in decision-making, assuring that the woman has a safe place to stay following the rape. By serving as an intermediary, the advocate can ease the pain of coping with the rape and help the woman identify her needs after the rape. The advocate usually begins her involvement with the victim when a call is placed to the police or a local women's center indicating that a rape has occurred. The advocate usually meets the woman at the hospital and will continue to work with her through the trial process if she desires.

In some communities, rape crisis centers will send a team of rape advocates. Often one member of the team will stay with the victim and help meet her needs, while the other member will deal with family members or friends who may be with the woman. This advocate will help significant others find ways that they can be useful to the victim as well as helping these individuals deal with their own feelings.

Rosalie Taylor, as one of the founders of the Oklahoma City crisis line, has been involved with numerous rape cases that were in fact brought to trial. The following discussion is based on her observations and experiences with the judicial process in the state of Oklahoma.

Most rape victims have had little experience with courtrooms and the legal process. Much of what a woman imagines occurring in the courtroom is based on perceptions which have often been shaped by television, movies and other forms of media. Realistically, her idea of what might occur and what actually does occur are two different scenarios. Thus, the victim is dealing not only with her present situation but also a myriad of assumptions based on her images of what she might expect.

Often, women feel defensive when questioned by the police. They feel that the police will be judgmental and blame them in some way for the rape. As victims, women often feel helpless when dealing with the police. There's always the question, "Will they believe me?" In some states, rape victims are required to take a polygraph test before the police continue with the investigation. Again, by asking a woman to submit to such a test, her experience is questioned. This further serves to damage the woman's psychological condition in many cases.

The first step toward deciding whether or not to go to trial is actually made in the emergency room immediately following the assault. The doctor must collect appropriate evidence which can be used in court if the case goes to trial. If the victim chooses not to have the legal-medical examination performed, the physical evidence will be lost. Unfortunately, evidence such as semen and sperm samples, hair samples and bruises and scratch marks, foreign blood or skin, cannot be collected weeks after the rape if the woman changes her mind and decides to prosecute. It is, therefore, critical that rape victims be encouraged to go through with the legal-medical examination for two reasons: one, to collect the appropriate evidence needed to prosecute; and, two, to assure that her physical condition is attended to.

In many hospitals, there are designated physicians specifically trained to work with rape victims. They are guided by set procedures which must be followed in order for the examination to be valid as evidence in court. It is important to realize that not all doctors are trained to perform this type of examination. A family doctor may not have the knowledge or necessary equipment to do this exam. For example, one woman called her family doctor minutes after being assaulted. He instructed her to take a hot bath and drink a glass of wine. Fortunately, the woman had enough insight to know that she had been given dangerously inaccurate information. It was obvious that her doctor had little experience with rape. If she had followed his advice, important evidence would have been lost.

Once the medical evidence is appropriately collected by a qualified physician, there still remains the question as to if a man is apprehended and subsequently brought to trial. The next choice for the woman is to decide whether she is willing to identify a potential suspect. At this point, a number of reactions occur. Although she may feel a strong need to see justice done and the rapist put behind bars, she may feel a resistance to follow through with the identification. She may fear the suspect's retaliation if she does make a positive identification. She may fear seeing his face again. It is at this point that the woman requires encouragement because of the pressure of having to make a decision about what she will do.

Rosalie Taylor describes this period as a critical time in the rape victim's experience. Her counseling efforts focus on helping the woman clarify the possible outcomes if she decides to go to trial and also the possible feelings associated with not going to trial. This allows the woman to see how she can regain control of her life by actually doing something with her reactions to the rape. It is essential for the woman to make her own choice and weigh both the advantages and disadvantages of the action she takes.

Identifying a suspect is not conducted as television has often depicted it. There is no line-up of men standing under glaring lights. Rather, the victim may view the suspect through a one-way mirror or identify him through photographs. In either case, her anonymity is protected. She usually will not physically come face-to-face with the man until the preliminary hearing.

The preliminary hearing is said to be one of the most difficult aspects of the trial process. The district attorney is concerned with several questions. Will the victim be a good witness? Will her story be credible? Will she be able to withstand the stress of the ordeal to follow? It is a most difficult and frightening experience for the victim. Questions can be raised during the course of the hearing which will not be admissible in the trial itself. Accusations concerning a woman's morals or sexual experience are often raised in an effort to rattle the woman's testimony. Often in the preliminary hearing, the woman feels like she is the one being prosecuted for a crime. Both attorneys are sizing her up to see how strong her testimony is and how strong a witness she will be. If the attorneys feel that there is enough evidence to go to trial, the case will proceed. In addition, since this is the first time she will be face-to-face with the rapist, a great deal of anxiety is generated. Seeing the rapist again can be unnerving to the woman. Therefore, it is paramount that a woman know what to expect before she enters the hearing. She must be given adequate information during this aspect of the process. The woman must understand why the attorneys are questioning her and the purpose of the hearing itself.

After the hearing, the advocate may need to help the woman deal with the feelings which were raised during the hearing. The woman might, in fact, resist going to trial based on her experience at the hearing. She needs the encouragement of the advocate as well as the knowledge that the trial will not be as grueling as the hearing.

At this time, too, the advocate should help the woman clarify who she would like to be present at the hearing and trial. There may be certain friends or family members whose presence at the trial would be beneficial while there may be some individuals who would only aggravate the situation for her. Thus, the advocate can serve to help identify the victim's specific needs and help the women prepare for the trial which will follow.

The jury plays a critical role in the trial itself. The victim should be aware that the suspect might be instructed by his lawyer to play on the jurors' perceptions and misinformation concerning rape. The suspect might attend the trial in a suit, looking very respectable. This ploy is used to deceive the jurors into thinking that the defendant couldn't possibly be a rapist. All too many people imagine a rapist as an individual with less socially disirable characteristics. A woman must be aware that this type of psychological warfare does go on in the courtroom. Women should be prepared for this tactic.

In one case, a woman was raped by a desk clerk at a motel where she was staying. The desk clerk used a passkey to break into her room. At the trial, the man looked quite respectable and presented himself in a congenial manner. His wife, who was eight months pregnant, was seated near his side. This was obviously a strategy used by the defendant's lawyer to affect the final decision by the jury. Fortunately, the jury was not swayed by this display and the man was convicted.

A woman must also be aware of the image she presents in the courtroom. Many jurors still believe that a woman still asks for "it." A woman must be clear about the type of impression she wants to make on the jury. Because of the biases of jury members, the rape advocate needs to spend a good deal of time discussing this reality and helping the woman prepare to deal with archaic attitudes. The woman's manner of dress, use of language and choice of words can reinforce or change stereotypes held by jurors. For example, one woman was told she lost the case because she used a number of slang words when referring to body parts in her description of the rape. Her particular choice of words served to confirm the juries biases that she was a "loose" woman.

Above all else, it is essential that a woman be honest throughout the trial. In another case, a woman was being cross-examined by the defense attorney. He had insinuated that she had been coached in how to respond while on the stand. The woman replied, "I was told to be honest." This response gave her much needed credibility in the eyes of the court.

On a psychological level, the trial serves several important functions aside from the criminal prosecution aspect. It helps the woman regain some control in her life by taking positive action. By going to trial, she can begin to move out of a "victim" role and take the situation into her own hands. By having to describe her experience in detail in front of the judge, jury, attorneys, accused rapist and others, she is forced to examine aspects of the rape and feelings associated to it that she may have repressed. The trial process, then, serves as a forum to enable her to work through some of her hidden feelings about the rape. With a rape advocate's help, this can be a very powerful counseling experience. Feelings of anger, shame and guilt will surface and can be dealt with at this time. Without the trial, the victim must find other ways to work through the emotions associated with the rape after-math. The trial forces her to do this. The trial also can serve as a symbolic ending to the rape. The man has been caught, taken to court and, hopefully, sentenced for his crime.

Many women who do not go to trial experience a feeling of incompleteness as if a part of the experience is unfinished. The need for closure is essential. The trial process serves this function.

A woman must also explore the possibility of how she'll respond if the man is found not guilty or if the sentence given is light. This is important to address because much of the case rests on the attorneys' presentation, the jurors' attitudes and the ideologies of the judge. Part of the painful learning here may be that justice is not always served. In one case, a man was found not guilty because the juror believe that the only way a woman could be raped was if she was unconscious. Even though the woman had been tied up during the assault, the juror was still not convinced that this was rape.

The rape advocate then has the role of guiding a wo-man through various aspects of the healing process. The advocate can encourage a woman to go to trial as one way for her to regain some of her lost power, to address unresolved feelings about the rape and to try to assure that one less rapist walks the street. The advocate can help the woman clarify questions concerning the hearing and trial process, how to deal with the courtroom experience, and what she might expect to take place during the trial. Another way the advocate can help the victim is to take the victim to the courtroom before the trial and let her physically become familiar with the courtroom surroundings. This helps relieve some of the anxiety that she might experience.

The outcome of the trial go beyond whether or not the man gets convicted for rape and the helpful psychological effects. The trial process also enables the woman to see who is willing to stand by her. Those relationships that are un-stable will suffer and eventually terminate. Thus, the trial highlights key aspects of a woman's life and serves as a basis of reflection for not only her rape experience but also other components of her life as well. In one case, a woman was admonished by her husband for crying while on the witness stand. He showed little empathy for her pain and the difficulty of the experience. The outcome of his response was divorce several months later.

Fortunately, some changes are taking place in the legal realm to make it easier for women in court. Many state laws are being changed which recognize the reality of rape as sexual assault. The use of a woman's sexual history, for example, is no longer relevant in most states. Some states are considering rape in marital situations as well. States such as Michigan have gone well beyond traditional ines in their definition of what constitutes sexual assault. In other states, sexual assault is no longer applicable to women only.

Special attorneys are also being designated to work on rape cases. This has created an important change in the judicial process. Previously, inexperienced attorneys would often be assigned to work rape cases. They would not have the background or experience necessary to effectively deal with the case. Often, attorneys did not want to take on a rape case because they perceived that such a case would have a negative effect on their career. Many lawyers fear the emotionality of such cases because of their own lack of awareness and their own internalized attitudes and fears about rape. However, some major strides have been made in the presentation of rape cases. For example, in San Diego, lawyers are now using "expert witnesses" on behalf of the rape victim as part of their court presentation. These witnesses serve to reeducate the jury about possible reactions of women in rape situations. The expert is often someone who has information and data that can be used to help the victim support her actions during the rape itself. The expert witness describes the current literature, films and other media which encourage a woman not to resist unless she can safely escape the assailant. This type of information enables the jurors to better understand why a woman might not fight back. It also gives her behavior credibility in the eyes of the court and serves to reinforce her own actions related to the actual assault. With this type of information, the jurors might see the victim's behavior from a more realistic perspective.

The expert witness can also testify concerning the effects of rape on the victim. By discussing rape trauma syndrome and examining a woman's behavior after the rape, the expert witness can establish the emotional reality of the rape and its effect on the victim. This testimony helps to assert that a rape did, in fact, occur. This type of help is particularly useful in the case of an acquaintance rape when evidence is sometimes difficult to obtain.

The expert witness, then, performs several functions. The individual can corroborate and give credibility to the victim's testimony and serve to educate the members of the jury about real reactions to a rape.

Although progress is being made, the bleak reality of the rape trial still exists. The changes in courtroom procedures and new legislation are encouraging but problems still exist. Rape laws and trials differ from state to state and from individual to individual. Women must be prepared for the courtroom and must be able to handle what lies ahead for them.

CHAPTER VI

THE LONG HAUL: COMING TO TERMS

Although a number of years have passed since the rape, I am aware that I haven't worked through all of the residual feelings associated with being assaulted. There are days when the rape feels like a very distant part of my life. Other days, it seems as though the rape has just occured. On those days, my emotions sometimes overwhelm me and leave me feeling very depressed. Hence, this chapter will examine the long-term phase in the healing process and discuss how women incorporate their reactions into their daily living.

At this point, the rape no longer controls a woman's feelings or thoughts. Whereas in the previous short-term stage, a woman feels as if she is constantly reacting to the rape. In this phase, the woman now begins to have more control over her reactions and responses. It is through this regaining of control that the woman begins to regain and reestablish a sense of power. This sense of power includes feeling comfortable with oneself, an ability to recognize the strength one has in surviving the rape, and an ability to incorporate the experience into one's life. The rape no longer is the fundamental core around which one's life is built. It is important to realize that the long-term integration can take several years.

In many ways, time heal wounds but it is naive to

think that time alone will make the feelings vanish. Time, coupled with actively dealing with a woman's reaction, is essential to the rape along each step of the way. In my case, it was almost three years after the assault before I felt comfortable with myself. I no longer thought about the rape on a daily basis. The feelings of paranoia and extreme anxiety began to dissipate.

Initially following the rape and in the months and years after that, I found myself needing to discuss the rape with friends. Now this need had changed. In the long-term phase, I found that I could share the experience with others when it felt appropriate. The rape no longer consumed all of my energy. It no longer controlled my life. When meeting other people, the rape ceased to be the focal point of our conversation. I found that when I did share information about the rape with new friends, it was in the context of sharing experiences with another person. I do not want to hide the fact that I was raped but the disclosure has to be appropriate to the conversation and the individual with whom I'm dealing.

Those people that I am close to need to be aware of the impact of the rape on my life. Clearly, I am not the same person I was before the rape. The impact has been profound and in some ways scars are lasting. Friends must recognize that such a trauma cannot be easily forgotten. Their support and understanding is needed since, at times, unresolved issues surface unexpectedly. My reactions now are much less overt than they were previously. I may, for example, hear that someone has been raped in the community and find myself, several hours later, experiencing a headache, tight stomach, anxiety or anger. Often I do not recognize initially that I am responding to the rape both for that woman and myself. It is only when I trace back events of the day do I connect the effect my being raped still has on me.

One major aspect of coming to terms with being raped is that I have regained a sense of power in my life. Surviving this life-threatening situation, both in terms of the assault itself and the hell of the aftermath, has enabled me to recognize the internal resources I have. I feel that if I could survive the rape, and all the feelings associated with it, I can survive just about anything. I also see now that the action I took during the rape; i.e., talking to the rapist, asking him questions, were my survival skills. I no longer blame myself or feel shameful for my actions. I have faced, throughout these years, immense loneliness and the possibility of death. Through this, I have come to terms with the fact that basically I am alone in the world. Coupled with this learning is the awareness that I can seek out and identify the resources I need to help myself. I feel stronger now knowing that I can ask for what I need. I can also recognize a choice, for example, of living with a man as a choice made freely rather than as a reaction to the rape. All of this has helped me to identify a new sense of internal power that exists within myself.

I am aware of having a much deeper sensitivity to the pain experienced by others. All of what has happened to me has further opened my eyes to the gap which exists between women and men. I now have a better understanding of how difficult it is for most men to relate to a woman who has been raped. I am also aware of why women who have not been raped may want to deny another woman's experience. I'm also more sensitive to other women who have had the same experience.

One way that I have tried to use my experience to help others is to be open and public about being raped. My professional position as a University professor involved in the human relations and counseling fields has given me a forum to openly address the issue of rape. In 1978, I was invited to give a presentation at the statewide conference on Violence Against Women. Up until that time, I had only talked with friends and acquaintances about being assaulted. At the conference, I related my experience much as I have done here in terms of reactions to the assault, needs that I had and what behaviors from friends and family helped and hindered my dealing with the rape. There was a great deal of encouragement from the participants. I began the presentation by telling people that part of the objective of the session was to be able to ask questions that they wanted to know the answers to but usually were afraid to ask of a woman who had been raped. I felt in this way I could perhaps break down some of the myths that people hold or help others who may feel helpless when someone close to them has been raped.

There was an obvious difference in the types of questions people asked. Some, it appeared, were very knowledgeable about rape; whereas others seemed to have strongly internalized the myths of rape. By answering questions, I was able to dispel some of those beliefs. Some people expressed feelings of helplessness when someone close to them had been raped. Several people were concerned about how to let their friend know they were there to help her, yet not make her feel pushed or as if they were prying. Others remarked that they wanted to help but did not know how. My response to these individuals was that they needed to honestly express these feelings to the woman so that she could let them know how they could help. That, too, would give her the choice. As I gave my presentation, I made a point of watching the reactions of the women in the audience. Some would nod in a knowing way. Often, these women were the ones who asked questions which subtly indicated their own experience with rape. Some women came up to me after the session and shared their appreciation. They needed to make contact as a way of saying, "I understand what you're talking about." The head nods, questions and statements of these women were ways for them to acknowledge their own experience as rape victims.

I have continued to speak to university classes, sororities, community groups and local media concerning rape as a political issue and my own experience. By talking about rape publicly, I feel that I lend my support to other victims and raise the awareness of the community that rape is a reality. In addition, it has been still another way for me to work through some of my feelings. For example, at each presentation I find different aspects of the experience become easier to discuss as time passes.

The response that I have received from different groups on campus has been extremely interesting. I've spoken to groups which vary from women's studies classes, made up mainly of women, to health and recreation classes, consisting of mostly male athletic team members. In each class I usually hand out an information survey in which I ask students to anonymously indicate: (1) If they have ever been raped; (2) If they know anyone who has been raped; and (3) To identify questions they might have about rape. An analysis of the data gathered thus far indicates that usually 10 percent of the female students have been assaulted and 30 percent of the students know a friend, family member or acquaintance who has been raped.

In these classes, the responses vary. Some students ask questions centering around how to help a friend or roommate who has been attacked. Often, female students identify their own concerns and experiences with their classmates. Once the issue is discussed, students often share information about recent rapes that have occurred on campus or in the community that have not been reported in the university or local newspaper. Students have a great many questions; from precautionary measures; to why do men rape; to what kinds of political action can be taken to stop rape. On the other hand, some students have difficulty coping with the topic. This is often characterized by laughter, jokes and side conversations. I usually confront this behavior and point out the discomfort that is associated with the behavior. In one situation, a male student responded with hostility. He asked me if I wasn't asking for "it" by sleeping nude? I was definitely surprised by his question and found myself responding defensively. This was one of the more stressful situations that I have experienced so far. On the positive side, because of my presentations, both men and women have sought me out to discuss their own feelings or need for clarification.

The painful side of these talks has been the discovery of how many women have been raped and have not sought help. My discussion of my experience sometimes is the first time a women is willing to acknowledge the fact that she, too, was raped. The sharing of my reactions may bring back painful memories to some women that have been repressed for years. Many women who were raped in small towns, or by acquaintances, found nowhere to turn for help. Others described trying to get support from friends or family and being told indirectly that they were somehow to blame or that the individuals could not deal with the issue because it was too threatening. One woman described being raped by the minister of her church; another had been gang-raped five years earlier and thought she had adequately dealt with it but was still not sleeping; a third woman's sixteen-year-old daughter had been abducted and raped only a week before; another raped fifteen years ago had told no one--not even her husband. In each case these women finally found support for their pain. No, they were not crazy. Many had not sought help because they did not perceive resources available to them, others were trying to repress the experience, hoping it would go away. However, it continued to haunt them. My talks would serve as a catalyst to resurface those hidden wounds.

It was as a result of talking with so many women who had been raped and also in recognition of the number of rapes which were occurring in the community that I considered conducting a group for rape victims in Norman, Oklahoma.

In collaboration with Denise Fynmore of the Women's Resource Center, the first rape support group was formed in the Spring of 1979. When we first met, I found out that she, too, was a rape victim. We began our conversation by talking about starting a group for women. We quickly moved into sharing our own experiences and reactions to our assaults. Although Denise had a great deal of support in her own situation, she still had many unresolved issues to address. We were both able to identify areas which still needed exploration. I hadn't talked with another rape victim in such a personal way until then. We left our first meeting feeling secure that we could reach out and help other women in the community. This feeling of support and understanding was uplifting. Denise's work at the Center corroborated my assessment that such a group was needed.

During this period, Denise and I were interviewed by two local newspapers in order to publicize the start of the group. Our experience in each interview proved to be enlightening. The two reporters were women. Each one approached the subject of rape quite differently. One woman was very factual. She was concerned with the time, place, date and purpose of the group. It was apparent that she was having difficulty with the topic. The second reporter asked very different kinds of questions. She was concerned with obtaining in-depth information which would also raise the awareness of the readers to rape as a reality in the community. After the interview, she shared with us that she, too, was a rape victim. The contrast between the two reporters was indicative of how different women respond to rape based on their experiences.

The support group has caught on slowly. We have found that many of the women who are involved in the group experience are reluctant to participate. Some have expressed feelings of not wanting to attend the sessions and feelings of relief after they have attended. Much of this approach-avoidance is a reflection of the turmoil that women feel about facing and dealing with their feelings.

Women who have attended the Norman group are mostly white and range in age from early twenties to late fifties. Although these experiences differ, they still share common emotions and a common understanding of each others feelings. Each time a new member joins the group, there is a ritual of having her discuss her experience with the rest of the group. As she does this, other members of the group listen to how she is responding to the rape; they offer

69

her feedback on what they hear. The feedback serves to give the woman support and permission to examine her own feelings. The participants are able to help one another understand their reactions. Also, because each individual is at a different stage in her own healing process, alternative perspectives can be offered.

In one session, for example, women shared some of their reactions to the rape. They each shared an experience in which they thought that their fear was overwhelming. One woman thought that every man she met was the rapist. Another woman was unable to take showers because she had been pulled from her shower and raped. A third woman built a cement closet with a phone inside just in case someone broke into her house again. As bizarre as these experiences sound, all are true. By discussing out loud their reactions, the women begin to see that these reactions are normal in the context of what has occurred to them. To understand that they are not crazy and to know that these responses (also known as traumatophobia—phobias related to trauma of rape) are predictable helps a woman put her responses in perspective. This information serves to give her power. She can then free herself of worrying that she is losing her mind in addition to the energy she is expending in dealing with the fears.

The group also engages in problem-solving. Women help each other look at options they might have in dealing with significant others, whether or not to tell parents or children, how to deal with a judgmental roommates, and who should be allowed at the trial. These are just some questions which have been explored.

At times, group members have taken direct action, too. In one case, a letter of protest was sent to a doctor who had used inappropriate medical procedures during an examination. At other times, individuals have offered to speak to a group member's employer or significant other in order to give them more insight into what the woman was experiencing.

As leaders of the group, Denise and I may take a more active role and work with individual women on a one-to-one basis. At other times, the leadership is shared with the rest of the group. As time goes on, more of the women have been willing to take a more active role in the helping process.

A method that I have used to explore repressed feelings involves imagery work. Often I ask a woman to imagine what she would like to do to the rapist if she caught him or would have liked to do to him at the time of the rape. At first, women are reluctant to acknowledge their negative feelings. When trust is developed, they often share thoughts of wanting to kill the rapist or place him in a position where he would experience the kind of emotional trauma they have felt since the assault. This helps women to acknowledge some of the anger that rages within them. The group then presents a forum where thoughts and feelings can be explored. Once these thoughts are verbalized to people who truly understand, there is a sense of relief and freedom. Those repressed emotions no longer remain locked inside.

One of the major frustrations of the rape group is that the numbers are small. We know from police reports and conversations that there are many more women in the community who have been raped and who have not come forware. It is also clear from my discussions with black women on the campus that minority women in the community remain silent. Although the group is helpful for those who are involved, there remain too many victims suffering alone.

As a result of the support group and efforts of the Women's Resource Center in Norman, the local community has become more aware of the seriousness of rape in Oklahoma. However, there is still so much more that needs to be done.

Our endeavor to educate the public concerning rape has been helped by the local news media, too. One major problem, however, is that most talk show hosts are men. On one radio interview, the host held some archaic opinions about rape. I found myself, during the hour long program, constantly rebutting his questions and assumptions. He strongly believed that men were not guilty of rape but rather were set up by women who only cried rape later because of the guilt feelings associated with sex. I found myself firmly disagreeing with him but trying not to alienate the audience. During the telephone question and answer session of the program, most male callers shared the interviewer's perspective. The female callers, however, seemed to be more knowledgeable of the reality of rape. They were also supportive of my work.

Another interview on television did lead to a confrontation. I was asked to discuss rape and then field telephone calls from the viewing audience on a popular noontime program. The show is co-hosted by a male and female team. The male host has a reputation of being rather crass with his jokes and at times nasty. I was to be interviewed after a local physician discussed his philosophy on medicine. During the first interview, the male host cut the guest off several times, making uncalled-for remarks and jokes. Needless to say, my anxiety heightened as I waited for my turn. I feared that he would do the same thing during my interview as he had done to his previous guest. At a commercial break, he jokingly said to me, but loud enough for all the people on the set to hear, "I've been raped three times last week." He continued, "You know, I always tell my three daughters that if they're ever raped to lay back and enjoy it." I was furious. As I sat down next to him I grabbed his arm firmly and said, "I am a rape victim and I don't feel that rape is a laughing matter. If you make a joke about it on the air, I'll nail you." This apparently had its intended effect because he was very serious during the interview. Fortunately, not all the interviewers have been so antagonistic.

One of the most frequently asked questions, whether on radio or television interviews, is if I support castration as a reasonable punishment for rape. Oklahoma at one time had proposed legislation to castrate rapist. My response is two-fold. First, under no circumstances can I support castration as an appropriate punishment for rape. It deals with rape as a sexual act and not an assault. By castrating a man, the psychological and emotions problems of the man are never addressed. Secondly, if castration is the punishment for rape, many rapists may kill their victims in addition to raping them. I state, emphatically, that I can counsel a woman as long as she is alive; I cannot work with her if she is dead.

The real key, then, to stronger punishments is to first make the public recognize the seriousness of the crime. We must work on changing attitudes, behaviors, perceptions and laws so that the victim and the criminal receive their day in court. Only in this way can we see a real response to the needs of the victim.

At this point, I am left with a strong awareness of the reality of rape and the long healing process which follows. I no longer experience internal panic when I hear a noise at night or when a stranger talks to me. However, I feel a general sense of anxiety knowing I could be raped again. There are times that this fear is heightened because of the outspoken and visible stance I have taken on rape. I cannot help but wonder if some man will feel threatened enough to seek me out and "put me in my place." I am reminded of a quote by Susan Brownmiller that women can be raped at any time, at any age. I know I must be aware of this fact but not let it immobilize me.

There are times that I find myself tiring of doing talks about rape to different groups. Sometimes I feel like avoiding these presentations in an effort to leave the rape behind me. Other times I wonder if the speeches really do any good. However, each time I am reminded how much this is needed by the positive and negative reactions of the participants. Each time, too, another layer of learning is exposed for me and feelings to be further explored surface. The presentations and writing of this book have also served as therapeutic dimensions in the healing process. Overall, I have learned one important thing about myself during this period and that is I have the strength to make it through all of what has happened. If faced with a crisis in the future, I know that I will be able to meet it head on. It has been a long journey but it feels empowering to have made it.

CHAPTER VII

COUNSELING THE RAPE VICTIM

A sixteen-year-old young woman is sitting in a group therapy session. She is relating her experience of being raped by four men. The male therapist starts questioning her. Did you provoke the attack? Were you flirtatious? Did you lead them on in any way? Previous to this session she had been given a battery of diagnostic personality tests based on the psychiatrist's recommendation. The tests suggested that she was masochistic. Didn't you really enjoy it? The young woman breaks down in tears. The session ends.

If you believe this to be an extreme case, you are wrong. This type of behavior in therapy occurs every day. Unfortunately, many counselors have internalized the myths about rape. Counselors' values and assumptions affect their counseling mode regardless of how value-free they profess to be. Because of the nature of rape and its associated stigma, there are relatively few women who seek assistance after an attack. It is for these reasons that this chapter will explore the psychological aspects of rape and the ways a counselor/helper can provide genuine assistance to the rape victim.

Given the fact that few rape victims actually seek the help of professional counselors, psychologists or psychiatrists, it is essential to view the helper in general terms. The helper described in this chaper is defined as those individuals the woman seeks out for support. These individuals could be a professionally credentialed counselor as well as a rape advocate, friend or a family member. In each of these cases the kinds of responses and skills that the individual possesses will greatly affect the woman's ability to integrate the rape into her life.

There are several assumptions which must be made in order to effectively help the victim. First, the rape must be viewed as a crisis in the woman's life. It must be understood that her life will be disrupted by the event. It is also helpful to assume that the woman was functioning adequately before the rape occurred. If not, then other forms of help may be indicated. By assuming that the woman was normal before the rape leads the helper to focus efforts on the reaction to the rape itself. The counseling becomes issue-oriented instead of psychotherapy. Other issues in a woman's life are not addressed in crisis intervention counseling. The helper in this situation must also be aware of the need to take an active role in helping the woman. This includes initiating contact with the client, helping her set up appointments, going with her to the police or to court if necessary or talking directly to family members (Burgess and Holmstrom, 1977d).

Some assumptions are often made which are not helpful to the woman. To assume, as some researchers do, that the woman will recover from the rape in several weeks indicates a misunderstanding of how deeply rape affects an individual (Sutherland and Scherl, 1977). Not only does the process take a long time (perhaps as long as several years), but it is also important to recognize that a woman does not "recover" from the rape. Rape is not a physical illness although there may be physical symptoms. To recover assumes that one somehow gets over it. More realistically, a woman must learn to integrate the experience into her life. The rape will become part of her. In addition, both the helper and woman must acknowledge that she will not be the same person she was before the rape. Rather, the rape has created a change in her life and, subsequently, she too will change. These changes may be in how she perceives herself, how she conducts her life, how she interacts with others or where she lives. At some level changes will be made.

No one person can realistically meet all of the woman's needs. For this reason, I will explore some of the ways different helpers can be useful to the victim. Different helpers bring different perspectives and skills to their interaction with the rape victim. A trained counselor or psychologist may have excellent listening skills but may not adequately understand some of the normal reactions and stages that a rape victim may experience. Rarely do counseling education programs identify normal reactions to a rape experience. A counselor may, for example, hear the constant replaying of the experience as the fact that the woman is stuck rather than working through various levels of the experience. Or the counselor may see some of the phobic reactions to rape; i.e., not sleeping, ritualized searches, nightmares, as paranoid or neurotic rather than normal responses to a life-threatening situation.

In addition, the use of reflective counseling skills may reinforce her feelings of blame and guilt. For example, if a woman is describing how badly she feels for leaving her window open and a counselor reflects back to her, "I hear you blaming yourself and feeling guilty for leaving the window open," the outcome of such an intervention may be to reinforce those feelings. A more helpful response may be to enable the woman to see that the rape was not her fault and to vent her anger about the fact that she does not have the freedom to keep a window open. A counselor whose emphasis is on individual responsibility may also be reinforcing feelings of guilt, shame and self-blame. If a woman is discussing how she wishes she could have done something differently during the rape; if only. . .; and a counselor explores what she might have done differently to avoid being raped, this will only serve to further support her self-castigation. Rather a more active and helpful response is to focus on the fact that she used her survival skills in that she is alive to talk about the rape. Helping her identify in what ways she used her power may serve to empower her. The counselor then must have not only adequate skills in listening and the process of helping, but also knowledge about the content of normal reactions and phases which the victim of rape will most likely experience. The helper must be willing to take an active role, both in counseling sessions and in the victim's world (Warner, 1980).

Rape advocates who serve as helpers usually have a good deal of awareness of the special needs of the victim. Much of the training rape advocates receive focus on normal reactions to rape. The training is designed to give the advocate the necessary awareness and skills to help the woman from the emergency room through the courtroom proceedings. Women's centers have done an excellent job in this area. Many rape advocates themselves may be previous rape victims. Here it becomes particularly critical that the advocate does not confuse her experience and needs with the victim's. One problem that an advocate may also experience, unless she is a trained counselor, is that she may not have the skills to identify when someone's reactions are not normal and needing alternative psychological help. The advocate may also not possess the skills to work long-term with the woman (Warner, 1980).

A third type of helper often overlooked is the woman's immediate circle of friends and family. These significant others may be the first individuals that the woman seeks out for help. The types of skills and awareness previously described must be considered by these individuals as well.

The ways that significant others interact with the woman after an assault will greatly affect the healing process. If friends and family members blame the woman for being raped, she will further blame herself and the healing process will be stifled. If she is taken seriously and allowed to talk about her feelings, she will more easily deal with the experience. Irrespective of whom the victim turns to for help, she needs to find an outlet to ventilate her emotions and reactions. Attempts to deny the reality of the rape and the associated emotional responses may be successful for a short period but repressing these will have a long-term effect on the woman and her relationships. (Katz and Wilson, 1982)

There are different stages or phases that a woman experiences in the healing process. These stages I define as: (1) the crisis stage, which occurs immediately following the rape; (2) the short-term stage, which occurs several weeks following the rape; and (3) the long-term or integration stage. Each of these stages will be discussed and the implications for counseling will be described.

The first phase of crisis follows immediately after the attack. It is at this time that the woman may experience a myriad of emotions ranging from shock and disbelief to fear, anger and anxiety (Burgess and Holstrom, 1977b). Her immediate needs are for her medical, physical and psychological safety. Often a victim's first response is the fear that the rapist will return. She needs to find some way to feel a sense of physical safety. The woman may be experiencing shock and disbelief at what has occurred. It is important to be aware that different women will respond differently to the rape. Some women may openly express their reactions to the rape while others will attempt to remain very controlled (Burgess and Holmstrom, 1977b). A woman may exhibit her feelings through crying, sobbing, smiling, shaking or a general tenseness or restlessness. The person who is controlling her response may appear clam, subdued or composed. In either case, the woman is reacting to the rape.

The helper has several functions at this stage. The first is to provide support, acceptance and assurance of physical safety. The second is to act as an intermediary between the woman and her environment. The third is to serve as a reality check to enable her to make decisions and help her identify the options available to her. As a way to carry out these functions, the helper must first attempt to identify the woman's needs and how they can be met.

The helper's initial responses to the victim will have a strong impact on the woman's self-perception. A primary emotional need of the victim now is to know who can be trusted. Because of the stigma attached to being raped, the victim will feel doubt and mistrust. She may wonder how others will respond to her now, particularly significant others. The fears and feelings will be tested through her interactions with individuals with whom she has contact immediately following the rape. Therefore, she will be sensitive to responses and cues which indicate trust or mistrust. There is no middle ground at this juncture. The victim sees others in terms of, "You're either for me or against me." The helper must give the unconditional support the woman requires. It is essential that the helper stress and reinforce the fact that first, the woman was a victim and secondly, that she used her skills in order to stay alive and survive the rape.

Support and acceptance are critical by other professionals as well. The behavior and attitude by police personnel and the medical staff at the hospital will serve a similar function in the healing process. If medical pr police staff are detached, the victim will feel more alienated. Particularly after such a dehumanizing experience, the examinations can be painful and add to already present feelings of humiliation. A physician, nurse or detective who appears accusatory or distant can enhance those feelings. An attitude of compassion and warmth, on the other hand, can help the woman feel more human. This is significant because in the rape experience the victim has been made to feel like an object, not a person. A way to help the woman out of that object role is for all individuals who deal with her to treat her as an individual as opposed to a "rape victim." (Burgess and Holmstrom, 1977a)

Another way the medical and police staff can be helpful is by sharing information about the procedures that they will be following. By knowing what will be done and for what reason, the mistrust can be minimized. It is also important to know that the doctor and police will ask questions related to the rape during their examinations. This is done so that the doctor will know what kind of evidence to look for. Often, if the woman doesn't know why the questions are being asked, she will assume that the doctor or police has no right to ask them. She needs to know the purpose of such questions.

Medical and police professionals can be helpful by allowing the friend or advocate to stay with the woman before and throughout their examinations. The need for reassurance is essential. The worst thing for many women is to be left alone in the emergency room with no one to talk to. The isolation and alienation she already feels is heightened. The rape advocate or helper can give the needed support, if necessary. In some areas police, medical staffs and rape advocates are trained as a team to handle rape cases. Both the police and medical personnel rely on the advocate to inform the victim of the procedures they will follow. In this way, the advocate serves as a mediator.

Other ways that the helper serves as a mediator for the woman is that the helper may take an active role. The helper may talk to significant others about the fact that the woman was raped or may accompany the victim the following day to the police department to file a formal charge. Later, the advocate or helper may accompany the woman to the pretrial hearing or to court if the case is prosecuted.

The third function of the advocate, friend, or helper, is to serve as a reality check. Often a woman is in shock immediately following the rape. The helper must help the woman find a safe and comfortable place to stay. Some people show no outward signs of emotional trauma and act as if they are ready to resume their lives as though nothing happened. The advocate must help the woman recognize the seriousness of the situation and encourage her to deal with the reality of the assault. The helper, therefore, must provide emotional safety for the woman so that she does not deny the rape.

Since rape is such a dehumanizing experience, the

woman feels a real loss of control in her life. Being in such a life-threatening situation may be the first time that she has had to face the reality of dying. Because of this overwhelming sense of loss, it is essential that she find ways to reestablish power in her life. Therefore, from the first, the advocate can be useful by helping the victim make decisions rather than having decisions made for her. Suggesting options from which she can choose a solution is one way to help reinforce her sense of power. Decisions from whom she should tell about the rape, where to stay or whether to call the police are all critical to her self-esteem and sense of control. In many instances, helpers who make decisions for the woman without asking about her needs only serve to overprotect her and to reinforce her feelings of helplessness.

The helper must realize that there is a fine line between support and overprotection which, if crossed, can leave the woman feeling as helpless as the experience itself. The key ingredient is to help her make decisions instead of making them for her. It is essential to provide alternatives for the victim so that she can make choices from available options. This puts control back into her hands.

The second phase can occur anywhere from two to six weeks following the rape. It is during this period that the rape begins to take its toll. The woman's life is controlled by the rape. Many physical, emotional and behavioral changes occur during this period in her life. In reaction to the crisis, a woman may have moved or changed her telephone number. Now in this second stage, she may develop phobic reactions to the rape. These reactions are also known as traumatophobia (phobias as a result of a trauma). (Burgess and Holmstrom, 1977b) For example, if the woman was raped in her bed, she may fear sleeping at night; or if raped outdoors, she may fear going out alone. Most women find themselves keenly aware of their own safety needs. They may put locks on the doors of their homes, secure windows and are extremely cautious when entering and exiting their cars. Others may ritually search their homes before they feel comfortable and safe. Some women, at this time, may experience difficulty with sexual relations with men. Sexual intimacy may create flashbacks to the rape. Other reactions during this phase may be recurring nightmares, increased irritability, mood swings or physical reactions such as vaginal infections or stomach aches and change of appetite.

During this stage, the majority of the woman's energy is consumed by coping with the rape. She will experience anger and hatred when she realizes that the rape still has an affect on her life several months after the assault. She may even experience great trauma each month on the same day the rape occurred.

Emotionally, she may be struggling with guilt and self-blame. The woman might replay the experience over and over again in her mind trying to see what she could have done differently to avoid the situation. If she is unable to express her anger she may feel very depressed and withdrawn. She is turning the anger inward and blaming herself instead of addressing the rage swelling inside.

The counselor, in this phase, can help the woman make sense of the varied emotions she is experiencing. The woman clearly needs to find ways of addressing her reactions to the rape without repressing or pushing aside her feelings and she must encourage the victim to do so. Because the surface issues of immediate safety and security are resolved, the woman may be reluctant to discuss the issue. She may feel that some of her phobic reactions are abnormal. All of this adds to her reluctance to open up and share her feelings with someone. Women sometimes feel that their lives should continue as they were before the rape but they can never be the same. Helpers must reassure the victim and let her know that her reactions to the experience are normal.

The counselor or helper must be aware that repetitively talking about the experience is not a statement of lack of progress in healing but an important aspect in the healing process itself. The more a woman is able to open up and discuss her feelings, the more progress she is making to integrating the experience into her life. Repetitive discussion should, therefore, be encouraged by the helper. It is imperative that verbal and behavioral support be given so as not to overstep the boundaries of the woman's needs for regaining power which are evident during this phase. The counselor must stress that the woman is responsible for asking for what she needs. In this way, she is put in a position to redevelop a sense of power in her life. The helper must also create the awareness within the victim that the rape is a part of her life. If done in a supportive way, this gives the woman permission to talk about the feelings, fears and reactions she is experiencing. Most of all, it is important for the woman to know that during this stage it feels as if the rape is controlling her life. She may think about it daily and feel as if she is reacting to it constantly. The woman needs to know that this is normal and find ways to cope with the reactions which surface (Katz and Wilson, 1982).

If a woman is not using the services of an advocate or counselor, she may also be reluctant to ask for additional help from her friends. On the other hand, friends and family members may be just as reluctant to ask the woman if she needs to continue talking about the issue. In cases of emotional trauma, the assumption is that the woman will talk when she is ready. This is far from being true. As a result, a stalemate can occur between the victim and those who could be of most help to her. This stalemate must be addressed in order for the woman to successfully heal from the rape.

The stalemate period is hypothesized by the author as being the most significant block in allowing the victim to integrate the total rape experience. It is, herefore, critical that the helper be aware of this dilemma and insure that the stalemate period does not occur. The counselor's availability and support must be reiterated frequently during this time period. In fact, a counselor may initiate contact with the woman as a way to let her know of the helper's availability. This is a different approach than traditional counselors might normally take with a client.

The third and final phase of the healing process is where long-term adjustment occurs. This begins at the point where no new traumas develop in reaction to the rape. It is a point where the woman begins to successfully integrate the experience into her life. In this phase, the victim no longer feels that the rape governs her life. She no longer finds herself coping with the rape on a day-to-day basis. She, now, can freely recognize choices in her actions and has found methods to alleviate dysfunctional behaviors. The primary difference in the long-term phase is that changes are made out of choice rather than reaction or fear. This suggests that the woman has regained a sense of personal power.

The woman at this stage will have developed insight into her feelings of self-blame, guilt and anger; and will be able to recognize the strengths which helped her survive the rape. The rape is now seen as part of her history and past experiences.

The woman may find that she has made many changes in her life and self-perception as a result of the rape. She may find that she has terminated friendships or withdrawn from family members who have denied the results of the rape's impact on her life. These significant others must recognize and accept the rape as part of her life. If they negate the rape, they are denying a part of the woman's experience.

The role of the helper in this final stage is to help the woman review the changes she has made in her life as a result of the rape. The counselor can help her conceptualize the process of integrating the assault into her varied life experiences. Part of this integration means addressing the fact that she could be raped again. This reality exists and must be confronted. The woman must face this fear without allowing herself to be consumed by it.

Those counselors who work with feminists should also be aware that rape victims may find conflict between new belief systems and old internalized myths about rape. The counselor must be able to help the victim come to terms with her feelings without blaming her or having her blame herself.

In conclusion, the roles that the counselor or helper takes are numerous. In addition to serving as an empathic support system and listener, the helper also needs to be: (1) an information source about legal, medical procedures; (2) a mediator between her and her environment — including dealing with her significant others, setting up appointments or going with her to the police or courtroom hearings; (3) a reality tester — letting her know that her responses to the rape are normal and giving her permission to address these responses; (4) an initiator of contact — including calling her, particularly during the stalemate period, to let her know of your concern for her welfare and of your availability to listen; (5) a re-framer — enabling her to transform her feelings and perceptions of self-blame and guilt to anger and power-lessness to control; and (6) a resource linker — enabling her needs to be met with available community and personal resources.

In addition to working with the woman on an indivi-dual one-on-one capacity, there are other services that can be very useful in helping a woman integrate the experience into her life. Developing a support group for rape victims can be a very productive way for a woman to work through her feelings of being raped. The other participants provide the kind of understanding which few people who have not been victims can offer. This group enables a woman to recognize that she is not alone and receive a reality check that what she is experiencing at some level is shared by others. The coun-selor, or helper, can be useful by informing a woman if such groups do exist within the community. Usually rape support groups are available through a women's center or rape crisis center. The groups are often run by a facilitator who herself has been a victim of rape and, if not, a staff member of the center will lead the group.

It should be clear by now that the rape victim is not the only one who is affected by the rape. The lives of signi-ficant others such as family members, friends, a roommate, spouse or boyfriend are also touched by the rape. Recently, counseling and helping strategies have addressed the needs of these other victims. In some communities, for example, rape advocates are paired up so that while one person works with the victim, the other person addresses the needs of the significant others who may accompany the woman to the hospital. It has been identified that significant others may experience many of the same responses that the victim does. These reactions include feelings of helplessness, anger that the event has intruded into their life and self-blame for perhaps not protecting the woman in some way. They may also experience impatience and denial, wanting to go back to the way things were before the rape. Therefore, the significant other needs some way to integrate the experience into the ways that individual interacts with the victim. The significant other must explore as well her/his own assumptions about rape and reactions to the woman who has been raped (Holmstrom and Burgess, 1979a; Warner, 1980; Peters, 1977). Significant others must find ways that they can be helpful to the woman instead of hindering her process of healing. Significant others also need to be aware of normal responses to rape and to recognize that there will be a disruption in her life. A rape advocate or counselor can provide this needed information. The significant other also needs support to explore his/her own feelings in relation to the victim and their own reactions to the rape. For some women, the rape may surface feelings around one's own vulnerability. For some men, their needs around wanting to protect the woman or their reactions to sexuality is due to the sexual nature of the assault.

In addition to a counselor or rape advocate working with individual significant others to help them cope with the rape, a variety of group strategies have been developed. Capuzzi and Hensley (1979) describe a six session group counseling workshop entitled, "Rape — Relationships and Recovery." In this workshop, rape victims spend the first two sessions as a group exploring their reactions to the rape.

In the remaining four sessions the woman can invite significant others to attend. During these sessions many of the conflicts which have emerged in the relationship of the woman and the significant other(s) are addressed. The purpose of these workshops is not only to reopen communication lines but also to enable both the woman and her significant others some way to see how the rape has affected them in different ways.

Some Women's Centers and Rape Crisis Centers are also conducting support groups for husbands, fathers or boyfriends or rape victims. There appears to be two very different responses exhibited by men toward the woman. These have been classified as a "traditional" view of rape and a "modern" view (Holmstrom and Burgess, 1979a). In the traditional view, the man sees that he is injured because the woman's value is somehow diminished by the rape. The man thus stigmatizes her and blames her for what has occurred. The more modern view sees that the woman has been hurt and treats her as a person in her own right. In a study conducted by Holmstrom and Burgess (1979b), they found that out of fifteen couples, nine men took the modern view of the rape and six men took a traditional view. These latter men felt betrayed, ashamed or repulsed; whereas the men in the former group were concerned for the woman's welfare.

These kinds of responses are addressed in support groups for men. These groups are designed to explore myths that the men have internalized about rape, particularly focusing on such issues as what might have occurred if she had fought back in cases where she didn't. This enables men to gain some awareness about why a woman took the actions she did. The men get a chance to describe what occurred as well. The ability to discuss the fact that a loved one was raped is useful for their own therapeutic process. Just as women need to talk about their feelings, so, too, do men. Part of this verbalization includes discussing feelings of anger, fear, helplessness, impatience, guilt and self-blame. It is helpful for the men to know that the woman is experiencing these same responses. However, although their feelings may be parallel, it is also true that the men experience frustration and, at times, are bewildered as to how such an event can change her whole life, reactions and perspective. It is helpful to remind him that there is no way he can experience what she is experiencing. Men need a place to address these and other reactions. In addition to sorting through feelings within their own support groups, couple's counseling can provide another therapeutic outlet for help. Unfortunately, most people do not seek out such services. Therefore, service providers must find ways to let rape victims and their significant others know that help is available. It becomes evident then that the counselor, whether advocate, friend or professional, can be a dynamic force in the healing process.

CHAPTER VIII

NO FAIRY GODMOTHERS,
NO MAGIC WANDS

There are no magic wands or instant panaceas to help a woman deal with being raped. Nor have we discovered any ways to prevent rapes from occurring. This chapter will explore some of the different perspectives on rape prevention, both on an individual and societal level. Specific information on what to do in case you or someone close to you is raped will be presented. Finally, this chapter will address some of the societal steps which must be taken to not only help rape victims but also to assure that rape will be less of a reality in our society.

There has been much controversy over what precautionary measures one can take to avoid being raped. Unfortunately, even the concept of prevention or precautionary measures is somewhat of a misnomer. To assume, for example, that if a woman follows specific steps she can avoid being raped assumes that she is somehow at fault if, in fact, she is raped. It must be reemphasized that even if a woman is cautious and follows every preventive measure outlined by police or other experts, there is no guarantee that she will not be raped. With this reality in mind, it is still useful for women to be aware and to do what they can to protect themselves.

Women must first face the reality of rape. This awareness includes the acceptance that, as a woman, one is vulnerable to being raped. Therefore, having bolt locks on doors is clearly a good idea. If living alone and on the ground floor, nails in the windows which allow the window to be opened only a few inches are useful. Initials instead of your name on your mailbox and in the telephone book (if your phone is listed) are also essential. In some cases, a single woman may use a different name in the phone book, other than her own, in order to protect her identity. Women need to relearn that they do not need to be nice to every man they meet or who comes to the door. Service personnel should have identification and you should ask to see it. This is particularly true in cases where you did not request service. Foremost, trust your intuition. If a situation does not feel right, get out of it. Although at times you may feel like you are being overly paranoid, many rape victims report that they had feelings something was wrong but did not listen to their gut.

It is important to be aware of yourself in your surroundings. It is not a good idea to walk alone at night, particularly in dark places. It is useful to find another woman or man you trust to walk you to your car or where you are going. In the case of another woman walking with you, you can in turn drive her to her car or home. Some studies indicate that rapists will attack women who appear hesitant, unassertive or vulnerable (Horas, 1981). Look assertive, strong and walk briskly if walking alone. It is also not a good idea to stop and give a man directions if he asks. It is critical to think of your own safety first.

Always keep your car doors locked when in the car or upon leaving it. Many women have returned from making a small purchase only to find someone in the back seat with a knife at their throat. Always check the back seat before entering the car.

A more long-term, precautionary strategy taken by women is to learn self-defense. Although self-defense measures can be very useful, a woman must feel comfortable enough to be able to use these techniques in an actual crisis.

Therefore, the learning must be second nature so that she responds to the attacker with an element of surprise. The woman must be able to incapacitate the rapist so she can flee or get help. For many women, learning self-defense means not only learning techniques in how to physically hurt someone else but also addressing the emotional conditioning process which says women should not be physically aggressive. This conditioning may be a bigger block than the learning of self-defense techniques themselves.

If you are attacked, the most important thing to do is to stay alive. Some writers suggest screaming fire if you find yourself confronted by an attacker. It has been found that cries of "help," or "rape" do not get responded to. However, screaming will only work if people are around or if the screaming frightens the rapist. There has been a debate over whether or not to fight back. Some suggest you do everything you can to escape in the first half minute—kicking, screaming, scratching. One study conducted at the University of Illinois indicated that fighting back works. On the other hand, law enforcement officials feel that although resistance may increase a woman's chances of escaping, it also increases possibilities of sustaining heavier injuries. My personal belief is that because rape is such a here-and-now situation, you must do whatever you can to survive. Although a woman may imagine what she would do if she were in such a situation, you don't actually know how you will respond until it occurs. Learning self-defense teaches confidence but you may also find that fear overweighs confidence in an actual attack. Therefore, recognize that each rape is unique and do whatever you feel you can do and stay alive.

For some, that may mean actively resisting through screaming, kicking, self-defense techniques or the use of some type of weapon. For others, that may mean using passive resistance techniques such as talking to the attacker to try and calm him, claiming to be sick, crying hysterically or telling him a boyfriend or roommate will be home soon.

Try to remember as much information as possible

about the attacker for police identification. After the attack it is important to get help quickly. You must first get yourself out of danger and to a safe place. Call the police, a friend, a doctor or a rape crisis line. It is critical to realize that even if you were not actually raped, these steps should be followed. Women who have experienced attempted rapes have reactions similar to those of women who have actually been raped. Do not touch anything, change your clothes, wash or douche until after you have had a medical examination. If you must change clothes, do not throw them away. You may be destroying valuable evidence. If you bring the clothes you were wearing to the hospital, put them in a paper bag instead of a plastic one. Plastic bags may absorb some of the bacteria and oils.

If you are raped, remember that the nightmare does not end when the assailant leaves. In many ways it is only the beginning of the nightmare. It is imperative that you recognize the gravity of the situation and give yourself permission, force yourself if necessary, to deal with your reactions to this violent intrusion in your life. Foremost remember, you did not commit the crime, the rapist did. You need to solicit the help of others. The feelings will not go away just because you want them to. Just as you may make external changes in your life as a result of the rape, such as moving or changing your phone number, you will also change internally. The reactions to the rape will probably control you before you gain your control back. The experience is part of your life now and your job is to integrate it and try to make some new meaning of your experience. Most important is for you to explicate your needs and to get help. Identify individuals who you can talk to whether they are personal friends, family or counselors and talk, talk, talk; whether for weeks, months or years, until you no longer feel that the rape takes central focus of your energies. Recognize that the healing process does take a great deal of time and energy. Even when you think you may be "over it," you may find times when it feels like the horror has just begun. You may experience the impatience and fury over an event that has cast its shadow over you for so long. However, you also need to realize that you don't have to be a victim forever. Each woman has to find the internal strength and power to integrate the experience. That is the task of the healing process. The healing process is a Herculean struggle in which the victim must confront the innards of her psyche and examine her every behavior in order to come to terms with her changed life.

One would like to think that this task has become easier because of the major shifts that have been made in society's awareness about rape over the last fifteen years. Although police personnel are receiving better training as are many hospital staffs throughout the country, a great deal of consciousness raising is still required. A recent study reported in *MS* magazine (Fingler, 1981) indicates that little change has been made in how teenagers view rape. A study of 432 Los Angeles teenagers indicated the "54% of the males and 42% of the females felt that under some circumstances it is all right to force a young woman to have sex" (p. 23). Results such as these sadly point out the fact that young men and women today do not see that forced sexual intercourse is rape. Obviously, we have not gone very far in debunking the myths surrounding rape.

Many of the myths surrounding rape must be exposed as fraudulent and accurate information must be disseminated. Assumptions, such as "Women ask for it," "A woman can't be raped against her will," or "A husband can't rape his wife" are all erroneous. We must come to grips with the fact that rape is an act of violence and not an act of passion. In addition, we must face the fact that it can happen to us if we are a woman, at any time, any place, and no matter what our age. The myth that only women get raped is also being exposed. Men have been raped, mostly by other men—in prisons and many as children. These victims also experience rape trauma.

In order to counter these myths about rape, a whole new relearning process needs to occur. Our society, through various forms of media, teaches men and women alike that women are sexual objects. Magazines, novels, and pornography continue to depict women as wanting to be raped. These media reinforce the myth that rape is sexual instead of the reality that it is a humiliating act of violence against women. In addition, our society continues to draw a fine line between what is sexual and sensual and what is violent (Brownmiller, 1975). For many men, sex is an outlet for their aggression. This feeds into their not understanding what rape is about. Because our society continues to perpetuate these myths, it is not surprising to find that many men cannot comprehend why a woman is so distressed if she's been raped.

Men and women both must learn about the realities of rape. Females are often taught as young children to be careful of strangers, never really knowing why. We do not discuss rape as a reality for fear of frightening our female children. Yet, because it is such a taboo, women have a difficult time recognizing the fact that they are potential victims and what they can do.

As part of this learning about rape, women must face the double message they receive about being female. Women are told on one hand to look attractive. However, they often get blamed for this very behavior if they are raped. Women and men must understand that regardless of how a woman looks, whether she be five years old or eighty-five, women are being raped. Indeed, all women are potential rape victims.

Men must learn a great deal about rape. Males must be educated when they are young that forced sex is rape. They must understand that it is always a woman's prerogative to say no to a sexual experience and for that to be accepted by the male. If not, the encounter is not sexual but forced, violent and rape. Men for too long have been taught to believe that if a woman says "no," she really means "yes." Men must learn to respect a "no" response. This is particularly how many acquaintance rapes occur. Women, on the other hand, must learn to take responsibility and say honestly what they mean. This will hopefully create more honest relationships between men and women if they can learn from an early age to respect each other. Obviously, this issue goes beyond the scope of rape to general dynamics of women and men in our society. Rape is only the ultimate manifestation of sexism and men's attitudes to women. We must be aware that rape is not normal. Although it is a cultural norm in the United States, there are countries where the incidence of rape is much less frequent. Japen is one such example. We must, therefore, realize that rape does not have to exist. Until women can walk the streets safely, day or night, or feel safe in their own homes, no woman is free in this country.

Due to the pervasiveness of myths surrounding rape, women are reluctant to report a rape to police officials or to share that with loved ones. Those women who do report live in fear over whether or not they will be believed. The cases most frequently reported are those instances where the assailant is unknown to the victim. However, here too many women are hesitant. Women who are poor or minorities often feel that they have a lesser chance of being taken seriously by authorities due not only to the myths of rape but also due to stereotypes of minority and poor women. Women who have been raped by acquaintances or husbands also fail to report for fear of being somehow blamed or not believed. Furthermore, in most states today, legally a man cannot rape his wife. These women who do not report remain silent victims attempting to deny the experience or repress it, hoping it will go away. Unfortunately, it does not.

For those women who choose to report being raped, there are services available to help. Women's Centers and Rape Crisis Centers are growing throughout the United States (Connell and Wilson, 1974; Peters, 1977; Horos, 1981). These centers are also found in various YMCA's and university campuses. Unfortunately, many of these centers are found in predominantly white communities. Therefore, the needs of poor and minority women are often not met

(Gross, 1979; Toure, 1980). Recent findings of the Law Enforcement Administration Agency report of rape in twenty-six cities found that minority women get raped at a higher rate than white women. It is apparent that much more attention to minority communities must be given so that all women have resources available to them if they are raped.

As a result of the Women's movement and Crisis Centers, awareness about rape has definitely changed. Due to this increased awareness, action is being taken. Marches against rape, often entitled symbolically, "Take Back The Night," have been held in communities across the nation. These marches are designed to let people know that rape is a reality, that people are concerned and to enlighten communities about the seriousness of the problem.

Men, too, are fighting against rape. Rape and Violence End Now (RAVEN), Brothers in Change, and the Santa Cruz Men Against Rape (France, 1980) are three organizations founded and run by men to combat rape. Their purpose is to heighten men's awareness about the problems of violence against women. They have been involved in consciousness raising seminars, providing child care for women, and offering counseling for men who abuse women. These endeavors support the fact that rape is not solely a female problem but rather a societal one.

Awareness training has been conducted with police, legal and medical personnel to develop their insight into the plight of the rape victim. Such training not only addresses myths of rape and procedures which need to be followed but also helps these professionals explore their own attitudes and identify helpful responses to a woman who has been raped. These professionals begin to see their role in the healing process.

Some states still define rape and the penalties in archaic terms such as Idaho's laws which date back to 1864. That law states that rape is "sexual intercourse with a female, not a wife, when the female is under age; when the female is incapable of consent on account of unsoundness of mind; when the female's resistance is overcome or prevented by threats of harm; when the female is unconscious or deceived. Penetration is required and the prosecution must prove force or violence. Corroboration is necessary when the victim's testimony is contradictory, her credibility impeached or her unchastity shown. Prior sexual conduct is admissible as evidence" (Bode, 1978, p. 236). However, laws of this nature are not the rule. States such as Alaska, Colorado, New Mexico, South Dakota and North Dakota describe rape in gender neutral terms, recognizing that both women and men can be raped. These states acknowledge that rape is sexual assault and further describe such assaults in varying degrees with differing sentences attached to each degree. Many states also have incorporated into their legislation the recognition that the victim does not need to show evidence of fighting back. Sexual histories are inadmissible. Great strides, too, have been made in rape laws in South Dakota where it is acknowledged that a married woman can be raped by her husband (Bode, 1978). Of course, rape laws are always changing. (It is important for you to know the current status of sexual assault legislation in your own state.) Although these changes are being made in different degrees in different states, it is apparent that much more needs to be done. Legislation, such as Idaho's, indicated how much further we need to go.

Attention must also be placed on apprehending and incarcerating rapists. Less than 13 percent of the men apprehended for sex crimes are convicted of sexual misconduct (France and McDonald, 1980). Unfortunately, most rapists are never caught. For those who do get apprehended and sent to prison, psychological treatment that works is rarely a part of rehabilitation. Very often, rehabilitation programs are on a volunteer basis focusing on self-help and individual responsibility rather than behavior modification of psychotherapy (France and McDonald, 1980). There is little research which indicates that such treatment serves as a deterrent to repetition of the same offense when the person leaves prison. Some studies which have been done in this area indicate that "four to five years after release from probation or prison, 25% to 55% of offenders have been convicted of another sex offense" (Furby, 1980, p. 32). Hence, much more needs to be done in apprehending and treating the rapist.

It is, therefore, apparent that so much more needs to be done to address the reality of rape in our society, both in terms of preventing rape and in remedial responses to victims of rape. It cannot be addressed only when it touches our lives or the life of someone close to us. Just as when a woman is raped, there are the other victims—her friends and family; so, too, the fact that rape occurs in our society in many ways makes us all victims. Although there are no fairy godmothers or magic wands to make the pain of being raped vanish or the reality of rape existing go away—there is hope. The hope is that if we can see how deeply this affects our psyche as individuals and as a nation, we can create a change. This hope is strengthened by the knowledge that if women and men work together, we will be able to assure that rapes occur less and bring an end to a nightmare that overshadows our existence.

CHAPTER IX

EPILOGUE

The first draft of this manuscript was completed in the Fall of 1980. Writing that initial draft served as a cathartic experience. I found it difficult to have to write every aspect of being raped. Each word would surface a multitude of feelings. In writing that first draft, I found myself facing many dimensions of the rape that I had thought were settled. Thus, I learned at that point of the many levels of dealing with rape.

Upon completion of the first draft, I found myself trying once again to leave the rape behind me. I would look for ways to avoid going back to the manuscript, fearing that other feelings and issues would resurface as I reread and reworked the manuscript. Finally, one year later I developed the impetus to complete the final draft. My fears that the wounds would reopen did not hold true. As I reread the manuscript, however, I gained new insights into my own healing process. I found that I described the rape as "my" rape. Somehow I was still owning being raped, that is, taking responsibility to some degree that I had been raped. I also discovered that in the long-term healing process, I had described feeling very anxious at times about the possibility of being raped again. Now I find the degree of anxiety has lessened. I also discovered that the issues related to the long-term process of healing were clearer to me when I returned to the second draft. This only points out how very long it takes to integrate the experience into one's life. Even when I thought that I had fully integrated the rape, I re-learned just how deep the wounds really are.

My friends and family have also changed greatly as a result of my being raped. No longer is it taboo for my parents to discuss their feelings about my being raped or rape in general. Recently a friend of my parents was raped. They were able to actively give this woman support and help her in ways that they could not have done previous to my experience. Similarly, my friends have drawn upon their learnings from my experience with other friends or professional acquaintances who have unfortunately been raped more recently.

Professionally, the writing of this book has created new insights for me. The reactions of male colleagues has been particularly revealing. Some colleagues have suggested that I write this book anonymously, given the sensitive and explicit treatment of the issue of rape. One was concerned that I could be brought up on moral charges for sharing the sexual impact of the rape. Another questioned if the information presented was generalizable to other rape victims given the uniqueness of my personality and position. That is for you, the reader, to decide. For me, these discussions have served to strengthen my belief that experiences such as these need to be openly shared so that we do not maintain and support the notion that this is an individual problem. The more I hear my colleagues concerns over the professionalism and merit of such a piece of writing, the more convinced I am of the need for such disclosure. It points out just how difficult it is to understand something outside of one's experience.

On the other side, the reaction from women has been one of support. Each woman who has read the drafts has responded that this book has had personal meaning for her. That is my intent.

Finally, I have considered over and over why I have written this book. Obviously part of the reason is personal, for my own therapeutic reasons; but even more important to me is to help other women who have been raped. It is only through shared experience, understanding and action that we can create change. That is the purpose of this testimony. For I am a survivor and the role of the survivor is to testify.

REFERENCES

Bode, Janet. *Fighting Back: How To Cope With The Medical, Emotional and Legal Consequences of Rape.* NY: Macmillan, 1978.

Brownmiller, Susan. *Against Our Will: Men, Women and Rape.* NY: Simon and Schuster, 1975.

Burgess, Ann Wolbert and Holmstrom, Lynda Lytle. "The Rape Victim in the Emergency Ward." In Deanna R. Nass (Ed.) *The Rape Victim.* Dubuque, Iowa: Kendall/Hunt, 1977(a), pp. 100-110.

Burgess, Ann Wolbert and Holmstrom, Lynda Lytle. "Coping Behavior of the Rape Victim." In Deanna R. Nass (Ed.) *The Rape Victim.* Dubuque, Iowa: Kendall/Hunt, 1977(c), pp. 140-150.

Burgess, Ann Wolbert and Holmstrom, Lynda Lytle. "Crisis and Counseling Requests of Rape Victims." In Deanna R. Nass (Ed.) *The Rape Victim.* Dubuque, Iowa: Kendall/Hunt, 1977(d), pp. 151-164.

Capuzzi, Dave and Hensley, Ann. "Rape — Relationships and Recovery." *Personnel and Guidance Journal,* 1979, 58(2), pp. 133-138.

Connell, Noreen and Wilson, Cassandra (Eds.). *Rape: The First Sourcebook for Women.* NY: New American Library, 1974.

Fingler, Laurel. "Teenagers in Survey Condone Forced Sex." *MS* Magazine, 1981, 9(8), p. 23.

France, Laureen. "Men Against Violence Against Women." *AEGIS*, Winter/Spring 1980, pp. 36-38.

France, Laureen and McDonald, Nancy. "They Call It Rehabilitation." *AEGIS*, Winter/Spring, 1980, pp. 27-31.

Furby, Lita. "Research on Offender Treatment." *AEGIS*, Winter/Spring, 1980, pp. 32-33.

Gross, Ella. "Bridging the Gap." *AEGIS*, March/April, 1979, p. 38.

Holmstrom, Lynda Lytle and Burgess, Ann Wolbert. "Rape: The Husband's and Boyfriend's Initial Reactions." *The Family Coordinator*, July 1979(a), pp. 321-330.

Holmstrom, Lynda Lytle and Burgess, Ann Wolbert. *The Victim of Rape: Institutional Reactions*. NY: John Wiley & Sons, 1979(b).

Holmstrom, Lynda Lytle and Burgess, Ann Wolbert. "Assessing Trauma in the Rape Victim." In Deanna R. Nass (Ed.) *The Rape Victim*. Dubuque, Iowa: Kendall/Hunt, 1977, pp. 111-118.

Horos, Carol. *Rape*. NY: Dell, 1981.

Katz, Judy and Wilson, Andrea. "Rape: A Case Study." *The Guidance Clinic*, January 1982, p. 6-10.

Peters, Joseph J. "The Philadelphia Rape Victim Project." In D. Chappell, R. Geis and G. Geis (Eds.) *Forcible Rape: The Crime, The Victim, and The Offenders*. NY: Columbia University, 1977, pp. 339-355.

Sutherland, Sandra and Scherl, Donald J. "Crisis Intervention with Victims of Rape." In D. Chappell, R. Geis, and G. Geis (Eds.) *Forcible Rape: The Crime, The Victim, and The Offenders*. NY: Columbia University, 1977, pp. 329-338.

Toure, I. Nkenge. "Report on the First National Third World Women's Conference on Violence." *AEGIS*, Summer/Autumn, 1980, pp. 70-71.

Warner, Carmen Germaine (Ed.). *Rape and Sexual Assault: Management and Intervention*. Germantown, Maryland: Aspen Systems, 1980.

RESOURCES

This section contains information about additional resources on the areas of rape described within this book.

Part I presents an annotated listing of several key books and magazines which address the rape victim's needs. Part II includes a listing of journal articles related to programs, issues and interventions designed to address the needs of the woman. These lists do not include resources related to incest or rapists.

Part I: Books and Magazines

Brownmiller, Susan. *Against Our Will: Men, Women and Rape*. New York: Bantam, 1975.

Brownmiller's groundbreaking work addresses rape as a sociopolitical act. This book is a classic for anyone concerned with rape. Brownmiller explores politics, the myths surrounding rape and presents an historical and societal perspective.

Bode, Janet. *Fighting Back: How To Cope With the Medical, Emotional and Legal Consequences of Rape*. New York: Macmillan, 1978.

This book addresses the emotional impact of rape as reported through the author's own experience as a rape victim and drawing upon case histories. The author also describes in detail procedures for medical treatment, police examination and legal implications. In addition, the book includes a brief summary of each state's rape laws.

Connell, Noreen and Wilson, Cassandra (Eds.). *Rape: The First Sourcebook for Women* by New York Radical Feminists. New York: Plume, 1974.

One of the earliest feminist books on rape, the New York Radical Feminists have pulled together a consciousness-raising work. This work addresses "rape as sexism carried to its logical conclusion" and the necessity to "speak out as an act of rebellion." The need for feminist and political action is also addressed.

Nass, Deanna R. (Ed.). *The Rape Victim*. Dubuque, Iowa: Kendall/Hunt, 1977.

This edited book presents articles by various authors well known in working with rape victims. Nass addresses problems encountered by the victim, mechanisms to assess rape trauma and medical and psychological treatment for the victim.

Chappell, Duncan; Geis, Robley; and Geis, Gilbert (Eds.). *Forcible Rape: The Crime, The Victim and The Offender*. New York: Columbia University, 1977.

The editors have pulled together a collection of eighteen articles which combine a variety of disciplines in both the feminist movement and the behavior sciences. Various studies are presented documenting how widespread rape is as well as exploring the relationship of racism and sexism. Overall, this work provides a comprehensive review of the research currently being conducted on the legal, medical and psychological dimensions of rape. An excellent bibliography is provided.

Gager, Nancy and Schurr, Cathleen. *Sexual Assault: Confronting Rape in America.* NY: Grosset & Dunlap, 1976.
This book examines the causes, nature and effect of rape in the United States. Gager and Schurr discuss the women and children who are raped as well as the men who rape. They also expose some of the attitudes and practices of the medical, legal, police and psychiatric professionals and the impact of those on rape victims.

Holmstrom, Linda Lytel & Burgess, Ann Wolbet. *The Victim of Rape: Institutional Reactions.* New Brunswick, NJ: Transaction, 1983; First Published 1978: John Wiley & Sons. Includes review of current literature.
Holmstrom and Burgess are well known for their work with rape victims in hospital emergency rooms. This book is a longitudinal study of rape victims from their entrance to the emergency room until the end of the legal process. The focus is on three major institutions—police, hospital and court response to rape victims and the impact of that response on the victim.

Horos, Carol V. *Rape.* New York: Dell, 1981.
In addition to giving some historical perspective on rape, Horos explores some of the myths about rape. She takes a look at rapists and some of the studies conducted on why men rape. The author presents practical information on rape prevention and self defense. She also describes explicit information on procedures used in case of a rape—including police questioning, medical examination, emotional impact and trial proceedings. A special section is devoted to the child victim. Information on starting Rape Crisis Centers is provided as well as a state listing of Women's Centers.

Russell, Diana, E. H. *The Politics of Rape: The Victim's Perspective.* New York: Stein and Day, 1975.

The author explores the politics of rape through numerous interviews with rape victims. Through these interviews the myths of rape are explored. *The Politics of Rape* helps us understand the emotional and physical upheaval that a rape creates in a victim's life. She focuses on the victim's perspective of herself, the rapist, addresses issues related to rape and race, and rape to society. Russell presents important information on creating social change, rape prevention and what to do in case you are raped.

Warner, Carmen Germaine (Ed.). *Rape and Sexual Assault: Management and Intervention*. Germantown, Maryland: Aspen Systems, 1980.

This edition compiles comprehensive information for rape victims and service providers to the victim. What makes this book particularly unique is the attention paid to victims who are minors, victims of incest, or male. This book is geared specifically for service providers and presents information on the role of rape advocates, ways to conduct medical, legal examinations and the impact of rape on family and friends. Warner also presents a design for continuing the education of those individuals involved in working with the victim.

AEGIS: A Magazine on Ending Violence Against Women. National Communications Network/Feminist Alliance Against Rape, Box 21033, Washington, DC 20009 (202) 265-9262.

Aegis is a magazine designed "to aid the efforts of feminists working to end violence against women. To this end, *Aegis* presents practical information and resources for grassroots organizers, along with promoting a continuing discussion among feminists of the root causes of rape, battering, sexual harrassment and other forms of violence against women." Back issues have contained articles on "Rape and Virginity Among Puerto Rican Women," "Taking a Stand Against Sexual Assault," "Building An Outreach Program," "Trying to Talk About Rape Prevention," "Can Rapists Be Changed? The Case of William Fuller," "Men Against Violence Against Women," "Why Women Do Not Report Sexual Assault," and "Rape, Racism and Reality."

Part II: Journal Articles

Albin, R. "Psychological Studies of Rape." *Signs*, 1977, 3(2), 423-435.

Allgaier, A. "Hospitals Respond to Rising Rape Rate." *Hospitals*, August 1, 1979, 65-69.

Ashworth, C. and Feldman-Summers, S. "Perceptions of the Effectiveness of the Criminal Justice System: The Female Victim's Perspective." *Criminal Justice and Behavior*, 1978, 5(3), 227-240.

Bard, M. and Ellison, K. "Crisis Intervention and Investigation of forcible Rape." *Police Chief*, 1974, 41(5), 67-73.

Becker, J. and Abel, G. "The Treatment of Victims of Sexual Assault." *Quarterly Journal of Corrections*, 1977, 1(2), 38-42.

Becker, J.; Abel, G. and Skinner, L. "The Impact of Sexual Assault on the Victim's Sexual Life." *Victimology*, 1979, 4(2), 229-235.

Bennett, J. "A Model for Evaluation: Design for a Rape Counseling Program." *Child Welfare*, 1977, 56(6), 395-400.

Burgess, A. and Holmstrom, L. "The Rape Victim in the Emergency Ward." *American Journal of Nursing*, 1973, 73(10), 1740-1745.

Bohmer, C. and Blumberg, A. "Twice Traumatized: The Rape Victim and the Court." *Judicature*, 1975, 58(8), 390-399.

Capuzzi, D. and Hensley, A. "Rape — Relationships and Recovery." *Personnel and Guidance Journal,* 1979, 58(2), 133-138.

Clark, T. "Counseling Victims of Rape." *American Journal of Nursing,* December 1976, 1964-1966.

Cottell, L. "Rape: The Ultimate Invasion of Privacy." *FBI Law Enforcement Bulletin,* May 1974, 2-6.

Courtois, C. "Victims of Rape and Incest." *Counseling Psychologist,* 1979, 8(1), 38-40.

Ellison, K. and Burney, J. "Dealing with the Victim During Investigation." *FBI Law Enforcement Bulletin,* April 1975, 13-15.

Freiberg, P. and Bridwell, M. "An Intervention Model for Rape and Unwanted Pregnancy." *Counseling Psychologist,* 1976, 6, 50-52.

Gage, R. "Programs for Rape Victims Applauded." *Journal of The American College Health Association,* 1978, 27(2), 67.

Ginnetti, Jr., J. "Counseling the Man in the Rape Victim's Life." *Nursing,* July 1979, 43.

Heppner, P. and Heppner, M. "Rape: Counseling the Traumatized Victim." *Personnel and Guidance Journal,* 1977. 56(2), 77-80.

Hilbermann, E. "Rape: A Crisis in Silence." *Psychiatric Opinion,* 1977, 14(5), 32-35.

Hoff, L. and Williams, T. "Counseling the Rape Victim and Her Family." *Crisis Intervention,* 1975, 6(4), 2-13.

Holmstrom, L. and Burgess, A. "Rape: The Husband's and Boyfriend's Initial Reactions." *The Family Coordinator,* July 1979, 321-330.

Kaufman, A.; Vandermeer, J.; Divasto, P.; Hilaski, S. and Odegard, W. "Follow-up of Rape Victims in a Family Practice Setting." *Southern Medical Journal,* 1976, 69(12), 1569-1571.

Keefe, M. and O'Reilly, H. "Rape: Attitudinal Training for Police and Emergency Room Personnel." *The Police Chief,* November 1975, 36-37.

110

Kilpatrick, D.; Vernonen, L. and Resick, P. "The Aftermath of Rape: Recent Empirical Findings." *American Journal of Orthopsychiatry*, 1979, 49(4), 658-669.

King, H.E.; Rotter, M.; Calhoun, L. and Selby, J. "Perceptions of the Rape Incident: Physicians and Volunteer Counselors." *Journal of Community Psychology.* 1978-9, 6(1), 74-77.

Kroll, J. "Policeman/Mental Health Worker: In Search of a Common Ground." *Innovations*, 1975, 2(1), 21-26.

Lester, M. "Rape: Why the Service Methods of Dealing with Rape are Part of the Problem." *The Times Magazine*, January 26, 1976.

Pepitone-Rockwell, F. "Patterns of Rape and Approaches to Care." *Journal of Family Practice*, 1978, 6(3), 521-529.

Poma, P. "Acute Management of the Sexual Assault Victim." *Journal of the National Medical Association*, 1979, 71(6), 589-591.

Robin, G. "Forcible Rape: Institutionalized Sexism in the Criminal Justice System." *Crime and Delinquency*, 1977, 23(2), 136-153.

Rose, V. "Rape as a Social Problem: A By-Product of the Feminist Movement." *Social Problems*, 1977, 25(1), 75-89.

Schwartz, M. and Clear, T. "Feminism and Rape Law Reform." *Bulletin of the American Academy of Psychiatry and Law*, 1978, 6(3), 313-321.

Silver, S. and Stonestreet, S. "Rape Counseling: A Model for Sensitizing and Training Helpers." *Personnel and Guidance Journal*, 1978, 56(5), 283-287.

Sredl, D.; Klenke, C. and Rojkind, M. "Offering the Rape Victim Real Help." *Nursing*, 1979, July, 38-43.

Stratton, J. "Law Enforcement's Participation in Crisis Counseling." *Police Chief*, 1976, 43(3), 46-49.

Whiston, S. "Counseling Sexual Assault Victims: A Loss Model." *Personnel and Guidance Association*, 1981, 59(6), 363-368.

GET HELP! More Resources from R&E Publishers!

NO FAIRY GODMOTHERS, NO MAGIC WANDS: The Healing Process After Rape by Judith Katz. There are no fairy godmothers or magic wands to help a woman deal with the aftermath of being raped. This book presents us with the author's personal account of rape and the impact of that experience on herself, her family and significant others.

$9.95   LC 82-61474   ISBN **0-88247-990-3**   Order **990-3**

BATTERED WOMEN, SHATTERED LIVES by Kathleen Hofeller, Ph.D.. *Battered Women, Shattered Lives* **presents practical advice** for dealing with **domestic violence** for the millions of women abused by their husbands or boyfriends every year. Case histories, guidelines for starting community programs, and the personality traits common to abusers are covered. *A Major Resource!*

$8.95   LC 82-50377   ISBN 0-88247-687-4   Order #687-4

RITUAL CHILD ABUSE by Pamela Hudson. This manual will help you discover the facts, treat the child and help in the healing process. A very important manual for all counselors, law enforcement personnel, parents, teachers and librarians. **A must for all concerned!**

$11.95   ISBN 0-88247-867-2   Order #867-2

IF IT HAPPENS TO YOUR CHILD, IT HAPPENS TO YOU: A Parent's Help-Source for Sexual Assault by Christine A. Golder. Finally, here is a handbook for parents who have had to face the horrendous ordeal of their child's sexual assault. It is typical for parents to feel as victimized and powerless as their child and the crisis can have long-reaching effects on the whole family unless help is found.

$6.95   ISBN 0-88247-768-4   Order #768-4

MULTIPLE PERSONALITY GIFT: A Workbook for You and Your Inside Family by Jacklyn M. Pia. People who suffer from Multiple Personality Disorder (MPD) were usually the victims of severe abuse as children. Ms. Pia is a ritual abuse survivor who developed multiple personalities. After undergoing many years of intense therapy, she learned to handle her own psyche and is now a therapist to other people with multiple personalities.

$11.95   ISBN 0-88247-890-7   Order #890-7

THE LITTLE GIRL WITHIN: Overcoming Memories of Childhood Abuse and Abandonment by Pamela Capone. She had everything—a loving husband and wonderful children, a good home, the respect and admiration of her friends and neighbors—yet she was filled with despair. Pam Capone was haunted by self-loathing, low self-esteem, bouts of bulimia and the memory of childhood abandonment and sexual abuse. This book is the story of one woman's struggle to free herself from the pain and isolation that had haunted her since childhood.

$9.95   ISBN 0-88247-901-6   Order #901-6

PERSON-TO-PERSON: Awareness Techniques for Counselors, Group Leaders, and Parent Educators by John F. Taylor. This book will aid counselors and teachers working with families or teaching courses in *interpersonal relations*. It is a collection of *activities* and *demonstrations* for use in supplementing standard lecture and discussion methods of teaching. **A must for all counselors.**

$15.95   ISBN 0-88247-738-2   Order #738-2

The Sexual Assault Survivor's Handbook for People with Developmental Disabilities and their Advocates by Nora J. Baladerian. Especially written for disabled persons and their advocates, this book is used as a guide and offers support after a sexual assault has occurred.

It works the reader through the events following an assault, and provides step-by-step guidelines for the survivor and her, or his, family. It can also be used as a training guide to teach people about sexual prevention.

$11.95   ISBN 0-88247-883-4   Order #883-4

HOW & WHERE TO FIND FACTS AND GET HELP $4.50 EACH

Rape-Sexual Assault	ISBN 0-88247-943-1	Order #943-1
Ritual Child Abuse	ISBN 0-88247-949-9	Order #949-9
Domestic Violence	ISBN 0-88247-942-3	Order #942-3
Sexual Harassment	ISBN 0-88247-944-10	Order #944-10